IN THE STEPS OF ST FINBARRE

Voices and memories of the Lee Valley

IN THE STEPS OF ST FINBARRE

Voices and memories of the Lee Valley

Kieran McCarthy

NONSUCH

*Dedicated to my parents Eleanor and John, and
those lost worlds in Farren Woods*

First published 2006

Nonsuch Publishing
73 Lower Leeson Street
Dublin 2
Ireland
www.nonsuch-publishing.com

Picture credits: Kieran McCarthy and Tony O'Connell

The right of Kieran McCarthy to be identified as the Author
of this work has been asserted in accordance with the
Copyrights, Designs and Patents Act 1988.

British Library Cataloguing in Publication Data.
A catalogue record for this book is available from the British Library.

ISBN: 1-84588-557-0
ISBN-13: 978-1-84588-557-1

Typesetting and origination by Tempus Publishing Limited
Printed in Great Britain

CONTENTS

Acknowledgements   7

Author: Kieran McCarthy   9

Introduction: Ode to the River Lee — A Pilgrim's Thoughts   11

I LOST IN GOUGANE BARRA   15

   1.1 In Search of Gougane Barra   15

   1.2 The Finbarre Story   19

   1.3 Creating an Island Pilgrimage Site   21

   1.4 Painting Gougane Barra — George Petrie   24

   1.5 The Candle in the Dark — the Tailor and Ansty   25

   1.6 The Free Country, the Unfree City   27

II FURTHER FOOTSTEPS — TRANSFORMATIONS IN THE RIVER VALLEY   28

   2.1 In the Heart of Uíbh Laoghaire   28

   2.2 Manoeuvres in Keimaneigh   30

   2.3 Unravelling Ballingeary   33

   2.4 Wonders of Lough Allua and Oileán Uí Mhaothagáin 40

   2.5 Inchigeela Narratives   45

   2.6 Times Passes — Religion, Education and Inchigeela 51

   2.7 O'Leary Homeland — Carrignacurra Castle   54

   2.8 Breaking the Mould in Inchinaneave   58

   2.9 Echoes of the Past at Kilbarry   60

   2.10 The Forgotten Country   64

   2.11 Remembering Kilmichael   69

2.12 Transforming Landscapes — Building the River Lee Hydro-Electric   72
  Scheme

2.13 The Gearagh — Landscapes within a Landscape   75

2.14 Further Footprints of a Saint — St Finbarre's Church, Macloneigh   78

III THE FUNCTIONAL RIVER   82

3.1 Macroom — the Frontier Town   82

3.2 The Aghinagh Way   88

3.3 Fortress Carrigadrohid   92

3.4 Coachford — the Crossing of the Coach   94

3.5 Inniscarra — Island of Friendship   99

3.6 Canovee to Farren — Toward a Pride of Place   102

3.7 Ballincollig — Home of the Royal Gunpowder Mills   109

3.8 Fragments of Antiquity — Currykippane and J.J. Collins   113

3.9 Carrigrohane — A Geography Inspired   115

3.10 Lee Fields — Journey's End   119

(i) Utilising the Pulse — Cork City Waterworks   119

(ii) County Hall — A Skyscraper to Catch the Eye   120

(iii) Our Lady's Hospital — A City within a City   123

Bibliography   125

ACKNOWLEDGEMENTS

book such as this cannot be penned without the support, input, time and patience of numerous individuals. First and foremost, I would like to thank my friends and family for their ongoing support. My thanks to Michael Carr, editor, Johnny Lynch, Dave Ahern and the team at the *Cork Independent*, where the sections of this book were first serialised. Thanks to Eoin Purcell and Kerstin Mierke and their team at Nonsuch Ireland for their vision and experience with this publication. My sincere thanks also to:

Tony O'Connell, Cork, for his excellent photography
Seán Ó Suilleabháin, Chairman of Ballingeary Historical Society
Derry Kelleher for permission to explore Carrignacurra Castle near Inchigeela, Co. Cork
Joe Creedon of Creedon's Hotel, Inchigeela, Co. Cork
Peter O'Leary, Inchigeela, Co.Cork
Peg and Tommy O'Leary for permission to explore Inchinaneave Farm, Co. Cork
Kathleen Lucey, Peggy O'Dea, Dan Hallissey, Eileen McSweeney in Kilbarry, Co. Cork
Ted Cook in Kilbarry for his tours of Carrignaneelagh, the Gearagh and Macroom Castle
Gobnait O'Callaghan and family in Toames, Co. Cork
Humphrey Lynch, Macroom, Co. Cork
Finbarr Crowley, Rooves, Co. Cork
Liam Buckley and Michael Shine of the ESB at Inniscarra Dam
Jenny Webb, Ballincollig, Co. Cork
Catryn Power, Cork County Council Archaeologist
Dan Noonan of Dan Noonan Archaeological Services
Prof. Robert Devoy, Department of Geography, University College Cork
Leo and Mary O'Brien, Carrigrohane, Co. Cork
Séan Kelly, Lucky Meadows Equestrian Centre, Watergrass Hill
Breda Harrington for her patience and insights,
And to all my friends for showing me other signposts along the way, physically and metaphorically!

Kieran McCarthy
November 2006

AUTHOR

Kieran McCarthy

Kieran McCarthy is a born-and-bred Corkman. He graduated from University College Cork (UCC) in 1999 with a Joint Honours Bachelor of Arts Degree in Geography and Archaeology. He subsequently completed a Masters of Philosophy (M.Phil) in Geography in the Department of Geography, UCC. Kieran has lectured widely on Cork's past in association with numerous institutions, in particular University College Cork, Cork County Council, the Cork Education and Support Centre, the Vocational Educational Committee and with various community associations within Cork City, and further afield in Cork's twinned cities, such as San Francisco. In particular, Kieran has a keen interest in disseminating knowledge about the importance of local studies in Cork's primary and post – primary schools. Since 2003, he has annually coordinated the Discover Cork: Schools' History Project (www.schoolshistoryproject. com). He has been involved in the compilation of several television reports for RTE on various aspects of Cork's history.

Kieran is known for his local history column in the *Cork Independent* (formerly *Inside Cork*), a weekly Cork newspaper in which he has been writing a series on the history and geography of Cork City and County since October 1999. In addition to publishing over 350 articles on Cork's development through that medium, he has published five books: *Pathways Through Time, Historical Walking Trails of Cork City* (2001), *Cork: A Pictorial Journey* (co-edited, 2001), *Discover Cork* (2003), *A Dream Unfolding, Portrait of St Patrick's Hospital* (2004) and *Voices of Cork: The Knitting Map Speaks* (2005). Kieran is currently working as a freelance historical consultant and can be contacted at mccarthy_kieran@yahoo.com or + 353 87 655 3389. His website is www.corkheritage.ie.

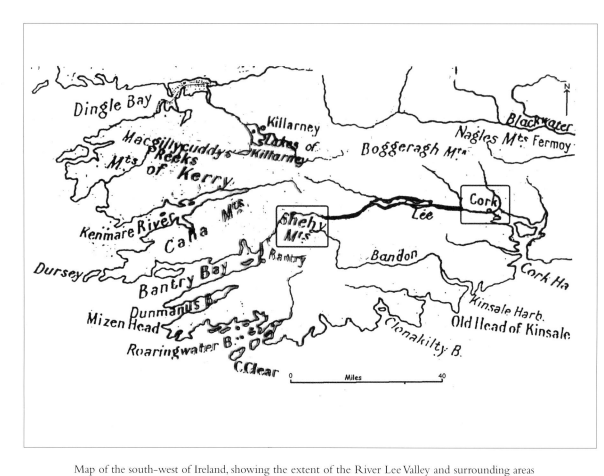

Map of the south-west of Ireland, showing the extent of the River Lee Valley and surrounding areas (source: Cork City Library).

INTRODUCTION

Ode to the River Lee — A Pilgrim's Thoughts

My first impressions of the Lee are from Sunday drives with my family to Farran Woods. The Lee Valley provided a chance to escape from the pressures of homework and growing up. Farren Woods offered an idealised world where castles and fights were dreamt up, bows and arrows made, and victories against imaginary foes were won. On those sunny days, the excitement of creating and defending an imaginary fortress was preferable to trudging into school every morning. I remember the radio on those Sunday afternoons, turned up to hear the results of the Cork GAA team winning and losing, and the associated cheers and sighs of disbelief as if the world would be a better place if Cork won rather than lost!

I remember trips to Gougane vaguely, with the Shehy Mountains soaring up high. I also remember in later years walking up the path in Gougane Barra's forest park with my dad, searching for the source of the River Lee and finding, to my disappointment, that there was no neon sign with an arrow pointing to the source but just a spring... well, a puddle! Perhaps it was from those early days that my love of heritage was nurtured by my parents, my Nan and my teachers. Those were good days and they provided a foundation for my interest in all things Cork. I was further inspired years later, teaching local history in Cork primary schools and telling children about the legend of St Finbarre and his walk down the Lee from Gougane Barra to Cork to set up a monastery. The monastery was the beginning of Cork and overlooked nearly twenty marshy islands, a canvas of landscape that in centuries to come was to be filled by settlers, all trying not only to make a living, but also to survive. I am always amazed at how St Finbarre, Cork's patron saint, is cherished even after 1,400 years. His myth endures and it is the legacy of St Finbarre that gives the city part of it core spiritual identity.

The origin of the name Lee is sketchy and is attributed to an ethnic group known as the Milesians, from Spain, who reputedly arrived in Ireland several thousand years before the time of St Finbarre. Legend has it that the Milesians acquired land in southern Munster — which they named *Corca Luighe* or 'Cork of the Lee' — from Luighe, the son of Ith, a Milesian. The River Lee, or *An Laoi*, has had many variations in its spelling over the centuries. In early Christian texts such as the *Book of Lismore*, it is described as 'Luae'. It has also been written as 'Lua', 'Lai','Laoi' and the Latin *Luvius*. An entry in the *Annals of the Four Masters* in the year 1163 AD refers to it as the 'River Sabhrann'. However, many scholars agree on Lee as the most common name for the river.

Sunny days at the weir in Ballincollig Regional Park, formerly the Ballincollig Gunpowder Mills (picture: K. McCarthy).

The River Lee and its tributaries drain an area of more than 400 square miles. The principal drainage is from the north from the Derrynasaggert and Boggeragh Mountains, while in the south the watershed is lower and supplies a lower volume of drainage. The Lee can be divided into three well-defined stretches. The first is the highland rugged section from Gougane Barra to near Macroom. The second section is the area affected immediately by the Hydro-Electric Scheme, encompassing Carrigadrohid and Inniscarra Reservoirs, to where the river meets the tidal estuary at Cork City's Lee Fields. The third section is the complex tidal estuary of Cork harbour. This book focuses on the first two sections and on the river's immediate path and the sides of the valley, from its source to Cork City.

The Lee Valley is one of the most beautiful landscapes in Ireland and has been witness to human presence for over 5,000 years. The landscape provides memorable, panoramic to intimate views, all woven together to create a tapestry of beauty. Ireland's recent Celtic Tiger economy has brought unprecedented changes in society: it has brought affluence, immigration and conflict between the global and the local. The Lee Valley has been affected by the architecture of the last century and the twenty-first century. The landscape has witnessed large-scale feats of engineering, from Inniscarra Dam and the associated reservoir to one-off housing. In contrast, the natural environment is still essentially rural, with a strong farming population.

The River Lee is an extension of city life. In a sense, the notion of a divide between town and country is disappearing. Places such as the Shehy Mountains or the pilgrim site of St Finbarre's Gougane Barra and Cork harbour are connected. Indeed, for many of us Corkonians the river provides a link with times past and gives us a sense of civic pride. Many of us have crossed the river's bridges and have appreciated its tranquil hypnotic flow. It reflects vitality, engages the senses and represents mystery and secrecy. Despite the parapet walls, the Lee is an accessible amenity that all can appreciate but which, for the most part in recent decades, we have largely ignored.

The geography of the visible river valley is fractured and diverse. It is a beautiful landscape, a landscape transformed through the centuries by people. The diverse archaeological monuments, from Stone Age tombs to the solitary Norman or Irish castle, to the nineteenth-century churches, demonstrate how the River Lee Valley and its scenery and resources have been used by its residents to nourish body and soul. The townland names on the Ordnance Survey Map tell a story — especially that of the impact of human history on the natural landscape. This impact was made over thousands of years.

For the majority of us Corkonians, the River Lee is an inspiring feature of Cork life, one that is sacred. It is a feature that each succeeding generation is brought up to respect, just like our other sacred places, like the Lough and Fitzgerald's Park. This work seeks to awaken interest in the welfare of the River Lee Valley. The history and geography of the valley is hidden and scattered along its sixty-kilometre journey from the Shehy Mountains to Cork City. The book is not a definitive work that covers all of the valley, but instead it attempts to highlight, discover, appreciate and explore an area through the voices of visiting antiquarians, historical societies, locals, maps and panoramic images. This work investigates the relationships between people and place that have created different landscapes within the River Lee Valley. It discusses the different meanings of the river not only for Cork people but also for those whose life journeys began elsewhere and who were inspired, like me, by its flow and the human and natural landscapes it influences. Moreover, this book is my call to encourage all Corkonians to go out and explore our own lovely River Lee.

Kieran McCarthy, *November 2006*

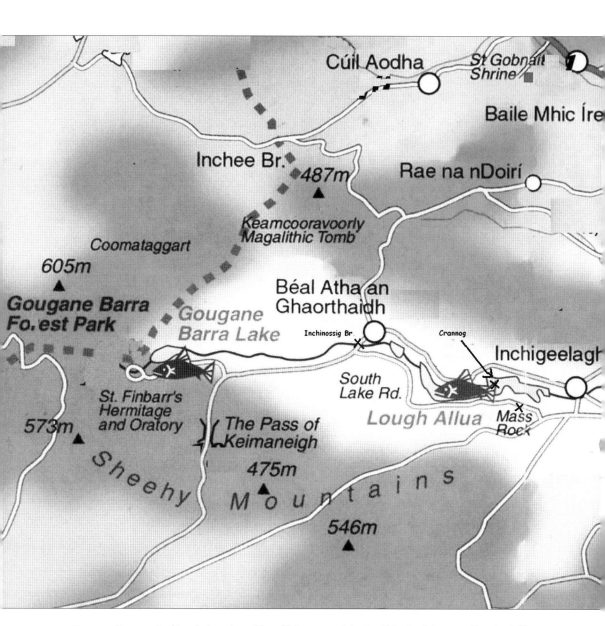

Gougane Barra to Inchigeela, based on *Map of Macroom and the Lee Valley* by Macroom Tourist Office.

I

LOST IN GOUGANE BARRA

1.1 In Search of Gougane Barra

A pilgrimage to the source of the River Lee is one frequently performed by two very different classes of persons, the superstitious and the curious; the first led by a traditional sanctity attached to the place, the latter by the reputed sublimity of its scenery. [1]

The origins of Cork, the 2005 European Capital of Culture, seem to begin in Gougane Barra with the legend of St Finbarre. Gougane has a notably mysterious but peaceful personality, which has seen and continues to see enormous investments of emotion, money and time by people.

Each person's impression of Gougane depends on their life experiences — unique to each person. For example, on one of my first fieldtrips to Gougane my main purpose was to take photos of the replica of the early Christian monastery. In the bleakness of that winter's day, apart from myself there were several families visiting the local graveyard and two swans waiting for their daily lunch from the sacristan, Mrs O'Leary — who was also hurrying away to arrange an upcoming marriage in the oratory. The rounds celebrated in the early nineteenth century as well as today (to a less rough degree!) are part of our common cultural heritage. The lake itself seemed dark and dangerous on that day and gave the place an aura of another world.

From the lake, the sides of the Shehy Mountains soar upwards and show the inspiring architecture of nature. The name Shehy Mountains translated into Irish is *Cnoic na Seagha*, meaning 'hills of the elk'. The mountains are an imposing part of the physical geography of the place and they capture the imagination of visitors and residents alike. They create an atmosphere of wilderness, myth and most importantly for many Corkonians, provide a sense of belonging. The names of the mountains all have a meaning. Each name, originally in Irish, harks back to a time when the Irish language was widely spoken in the country. Paper maps of local areas in Ireland were non-existent, and there was certainly nothing like the recent colourful *Discover Series* of the Ordnance Survey of Ireland. The names of the various local mountains in the wider Shehy range therefore represent the mental maps of local people from ages past.

At the south-east end of the mountain range, the name Dereen — *Doirín,* meaning 'the little oak wood' — appears in townland names, and it appears a further nine times between here and Inchigeela, even though not a tree now remains. Examples comprise Dereenacusha, or *Doirín na Coise,* meaning 'little oakwood of the foot, or bottom land' and Dereenglass, or *Doirín na nGlas,* meaning 'little oakwood of the streams'. The local townland Garrynapeaka, or *Gorthadh na Piece,* means 'wooded glen of the peak' and *Coom Roe* means 'red glen or hollow'.

---

1. Windele, J., 1846, *Guide to the South of Ireland,* (Messrs. Bolster, Cork) p.293.

Gougane Barra Lake amidst the Shehy Mountains, west Cork (picture: K. McCarthy).

Between the base of these mountains and the lakeshore at the east and north-east sides are the green fields and scattered hamlet of *Rosalucha* — 'the pleasant place by the lake'. Then there is the Pass of Keimaneigh or *Céim an Fhia*, meaning 'the pass of the deer', which leads into the Bantry area of West Cork.

Many of the mountain names above were changed during the Ordnance Survey of the country in the 1830s. This was a bid by the British government to stake a claim to Irish land, if in many cases only symbolically, by anglicising many Irish names. Pre-Christian residents in the Shehy Mountains may have originally invented the initial Irish names. There are a number of Stone Age megalithic tombs (*circa* 4,000 BC) and Bronze Age standing stones (*circa* 2,500 BC) in the northern valley of the Lee from Gougane Barra Lake to Ballingeary. The latter may have been in use for a short time, or they may have been in use for many years. Despite our lack of information on these sites, we know that the people who frequently used the sites for their own purposes would have known how to find the easiest tracks to access the sites. Their positioning was intentional and they were sites of ritual, either for burial rituals (in the case of the tombs) or in the case of the standing stones perhaps they served as territorial markers.

According to recent suggestions by Irish archaeologists, late Stone Age (Neolithic) tombs also date from the beginning of farming in Ireland and the centralisation of ritual patterns

Gougane Barra Lake and St Finbarre's Oratory with two of the residents (picture: T. O'Connell).

Keamcorravooly wedge tomb within the Shehy Mountain range with local residents Eoin McSweeney and Jack O'Sullivan (picture: K. McCarthy).

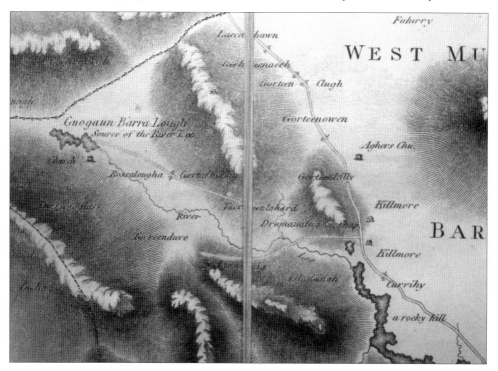

Above: The Grand Jury Map of the Shehy Mountain range, 1811 (source: Cork City Library).

Right: Gorteennakilla standing stone, Shehy Mountain range with Noreen Ring, a local resident (picture: K. McCarthy).

at local sites. The evidence of these structures shows connections with the land from an early stage in Gougane's prehistory. They also highlight the status-seeking nature of past local residents and the early beginnings of community. The Ordnance Survey maps of the Shehy Mountains do not tell the full history of the area. Structures such as the elaborate stone-walled field systems are located in the northern valley of the Lee, where the river leaves Gougane Lake. These boundaries may be remnants from the Late Stone Age and are evidence of the clearance of forestry or the practices of the first farmers of the area. The present human landscape of Gougane Barra shows us what kind of people we are, and were, and are in the process of becoming. Features such as Cronin's Hotel, the tourist office, the forest park and picnic area and St Finbarre's Oratory all provide functional uses for visitors to Gougane. They reveal that present and past residents of and visitors to Gougane Barra have all had different tastes, habits, technologies, financial means and ambitions.

1.2 The Finbarre Story

Artists like George Petrie, poets like John Fitzgerald and writers like Bryan Cody, Eric Cross, John Coleman, Seán ÓFaoláin and Bruno O'Donoghue have described the River Lee Valley in great detail. They have all highlighted in their own way not only the magic of what could be described as a carved-out rural wilderness but also the key transformations that the surrounding landscape has undergone. In fact, the personal narratives of Bruno O'Donoghue talk about the River Lee as a force for influencing the creation and spread of ideas on aspects of society, especially hopes and dreams

St Finbarre is reputed to have been the son of a blacksmith named Amergin who lived in a ringfort complex in the heart of the Gearagh. Today, Farranavarrigane, or *Fearann Aimheirgin*, is a townland nearby, which translated means 'Amergin's Holding'. Finbarre's mother is unknown but appears to have been a lady of repute from west Cork. Finbarre was originally named Lachlan, and legend has it that he entered a monastic school in Kilkenny early in life to be educated. His head was tonsured and his name was changed. Since he had a fair head of hair, Lachlan was renamed Fionn-barra (or in English Finbarre), or 'fair-headed one'.

According to local folklore, Finbarre was educated as a monk and established several churches in the Munster area. One of these monastic sites was on a rocky island in the centre of a lake

Depiction of St Finbarre in St
Finbarre's Oratory, Gougane Barra
(picture: K. McCarthy).

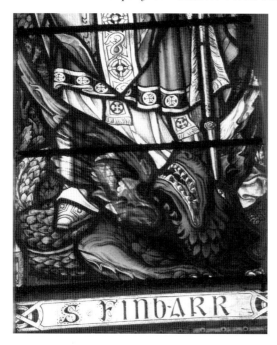

Depiction of St Finbarre in St Finbarre's Oratory, squashing the serpent in Gougane Barra (picture: K. McCarthy).

overlooked by the Shehy Mountains, where the River Lee rises. Indeed, the name of the lake reflects this: Gougane Barra means 'Finbarre's rocky place'. The details of the layout of that monastery are sketchy. In 1750, eminent antiquarian and historian Charles Smith noted that the original remains of a stone wall were present on the site when he visited. This wall would have surrounded stone or timber cells and a church and other domestic buildings belonging to the monastery in Finbarre's time. Based on additional physical evidence from another early Christian monastery, a replica of Finbarre's early monastery was constructed by Fr Denis O'Mahony in the early eighteenth century, and it can be viewed today. A large wooden cross within this present-day site is said to mark the spot occupied by Finbarre's original cell.

Over time, the generosity and general piety of Finbarre touched the inhabitants of the nearby area and many a traveller's tired heart. As a result, his reputation spread, causing his once quiet island hermitage to attract more enthusiastic 'disciples of Christ'. Looking for solitude, Finbarre left to find a location to establish a new hermitage. Hindered by the Shehy Mountains, Finbarre followed the easiest route out of the area — the River Lee. His search led him to walk the stretch of the River Lee from its source to its mouth, a distance of approximately sixty kilometres. It was at this point that he chose to set up a small hermitage on the southern side of the valley overlooking the tidal estuary of the River Lee.

St Finbarre's following the River Lee Valley from the Shehy Mountains to the tidal estuary of the river has inspired many stories that frequently appear in antiquarian accounts of Gougane Barra. Firstly, there is a story that tells of St Finbarre creating a hermitage (*circa* 600 AD) on an island in the middle of Gougane lake. St Finbarre is said to have battled with a winged dragon — that St Patrick forgot — that dwelt within Gougane lake. Legend has it that Finbarre chased the serpent out of Gougane Barra, a story that was remembered at the opening ceremony of Cork's tenure as European Capital of Culture in 2005. In the north channel of the River Lee in Cork City, a large puppet-like snake over 1,000 metres long was extended, over which fireworks were launched.

1.3 Creating an Island Pilgrimage Site

Centuries later, the original monastery of St Finbarre was a ruin and *circa* 1700, Fr Denis O' Mahony built a replica of it. The buildings that Fr O'Mahony built, the Pilgrim's Terrace and Church, still survive and have been preserved. In his *A History of Cork* from 1750, Charles Smith noted:

This lake is environed by a stupendous amphitheatre of lofty hills, composed of perpendicular bleached rocks, in some places boldly hanging over the basin. In some crevices of the rocks, grow yews and ever-greens. This place since the time of St Finbarre, has been frequented by many devotees, as a place of pilgrimage; and to get to it; is little less than to perform one. In the island, are the ruins of a chapel with some small cells, a sacristy, chamber, kitchen and other conveniences erected by a late recluse (Father Denis O'Mahony) who lived a hermit, in this dreary spot, 28 years…Round part of the lake, is a pleasant green bank with a narrow causeway from it to the island. That part of the island unbuilt upon, Father O'Mahony converted into a garden, planted several fruit trees in it, with his own hand and made it a luxurious spot for a hermit. Opposite to this island, on the continent is his tomb, placed in a lofty little house. He was not buried in it till the year 1728'.[2]

Through the work of Fr O'Mahony, Gougane Barra became a significant site of pilgrimage in Munster in the eighteenth and nineteenth centuries — and a major site for pagan rituals, which were eventually banned in 1818 by the Catholic Bishop of Cork, John Murphy. In particular, several hundred people made the pilgrimage to Gougane Barra every 23 June for the Eve of St John's feast. Antiquarian Thomas Crofton Croker observed the pagan rites in Gougane Barra in his *Researches in the South of Ireland* in 1824 of (abstracted from pages 275-283):

My first visit to Gougaun Lake was on the 23rd of June, 1815, the eve of St. John… For the last three miles, our road, or rather path, was up the side of steep acclivities, thence upon ranges of stone steps, over dreary mountainous swamps, and we were frequently obliged to quit the common track, in order to seek amongst the rushes for more secure footing…It was not without difficulty that we forced our way through the crowd on the shore of the lake, to the wall of the chapels on the island, where we stood amid an immense concourse of people: the interior of the cells were filled with men and women in various acts of devotion, almost all of them on their knees; some, with hands uplifted, prayed in loud voices, using considerable gesticulation, and others, in a less noisy manner, rapidly counted the beads of their rosary.

To a piece of rusty iron, shaped over a head, considerable importance seems to have been attached; it passed from one devotee to another with much ceremony. The form consisted in placing it three times, with a short prayer, across the head of the nearest person, to whom it was then handed, and who went through the same ceremony with the next to him, and thus it circulated from one to the other.

The door or opening to the front of the well was so narrow as scarcely to admit two persons at the same time. Within, the well was crowded to excess, probably seven or eight persons, some with their arms, some, with their legs thrust down into the water, exhibiting the most disgusting sores and shocking infirmities. When those within came out, their places were as instantly filled by others. Some there had waited two or three hours before they could obtain access to this ' healing fount' .

---

2. Smith, C. A History of Cork (Cork), pages 192-194.

The tomb of Fr Denis O'Mahony, Gougane Barra.

A drawing of the pilgrim rounds at Gougane Barra *c.*1840 (source: W.H. Bartlett's *The Scenery and Antiquities of Ireland*, published *c.*1840).

The pilgrim rounds at Gougane Barra, July 2006 (picture: K. McCarthy).

Gougane Barra Holy Well, 2006 (picture: K. McCarthy).

The blind, the cripple, and the infirm jostled and retarded each other in their efforts to approach; whilst, women and boys forced their way about, offering the polluted water of the well for sale, in little glass bottles, the bottom of broken jugs and scallop shells, to those whose strength did not permit them to gain this sacred spot. The water so offered was eagerly purchased, in some instances applied to the diseased part, and in others drank with the eagerness of enthusiasm. In the crowd, mothers stood with their naked children in their arms, anxiously waiting the moment when an opening might allow them to plunge their struggling and shrieking infants into the waters of the well. [3]

1.4 Painting Gougane Barra – George Petrie

The multitude of accounts of Gougane Barra shape the cultural identity of the place. In fact, 'Gougane' is a type of place that changes when you look at it, read about it, think again, then look again. Its different meanings and the reasons why people like to visit or live there come to the forefront upon further reflection. Other ideas about why this area is so important come from the work of the nineteenth-century Irish painter George Petrie, who produced a wonderful landscape watercolour of Gougane, *circa* 1831. (Image 13 in colour section).

Landscape paintings have always had a broad appeal in Irish art. They were the predecessors of the postcard. Many landscape paintings have become collectors' items. In a sense, they freeze, record, preserve and present important memories for the painter — more often than not of idealised worlds. Popular themes in landscape paintings explore the beauty and wildness of nature but also aspects such as the power of nature and its mystery.

Landscape painting developed seriously in Ireland only at the very end of the seventeenth century. Earlier it had existed only in the form of backgrounds to portraits or in connection with battle pieces, hunting pictures and similar works. However, in the second quarter of the eighteenth century it seems to have become popular very quickly. From the beginning landscape painting was associated with engraving, and until well into the nineteenth century, many a landscape artist made his living from engravings. These were often made for books, though individual prints were also popular. The increase in Irish country house building, notable in the second quarter of the century, meant that patrons needed pictures, including landscapes, for their interiors. They wanted a record of their new houses and estates. It was also a period when the first interest in natural landscape phenomena appeared.

George Petrie (1790-1866) was an important landscape painter of his day. Born in Dublin in 1790, his parents hoped when he was young that he would enter the medical profession. During his childhood, George had shown a taste for art, and so he was allowed to follow his inclination to become an artist. He was entered as a pupil in the Dublin Society's drawing school.

George Petrie assisted his father, a miniature painter, but eventually devoted himself to landscape painting in watercolours. In the early 1800s, George's work led to fieldtrips to Wicklow, Kerry and central Ireland. As a result of his tours, he presented many views of Dublin and Wicklow scenery — they were drawings in pen and in watercolour — at various exhibitions held by Dublin artists. In his early sketching tours in search of subjects for his pencil, the history of ancient remains, dismantled castles, ruined churches and crosses provided inspiration. In 1818 during a tour of the west of Ireland, he visited Clonmacnoise and copied the inscriptions on monuments and made drawings of over three hundred of them. From that point on he applied himself to the study of Irish history and antiquities. He began to explore people's memories and native Irish cultural traditions as he found them in the historic fabric of old buildings in the four corners of Ireland.

---

3. Croker, T.C., 1824, *Researches in the South of Ireland* (Cork), pages 275-283.

George Petrie *c.*1830 (source: Crawford Municipal Art Gallery, Cork).

In 1819 George Petrie supplied ninety-six illustrations for Cromwell's *Excursions Through Ireland.* He subsequently furnished drawings for several publications, such as the Rev. G.N. Wright's *Guide to Killarney, Guide to Wicklow* and *Historical Guide to Ancient and Modern Dublin, 1821,* as well as Brewer's *Beauties of Ireland, 1825.* Petrie began to exhibit at the Royal Hibernian Academy in 1826, the year of its opening exhibition, and contributed almost every year up to 1858. He was elected an Associate of the Academy on 9 May 1826 and a Member on 12 May 1828. Up to this time no painter who confined himself to work in watercolour had been made a full member.

In October 1857, the general body of members at the academy elected Petrie as Academy President. His work may be studied in the representative collection in the National Gallery of Ireland, which contains several drawings considered masterpieces in his day. Today, Petrie is remembered for an array of talents not only as a painter but also as an academic, antiquarian, archaeologist, historian and musicologist.

Petrie's painting entitled 'Gougane Barra with the Hermitage of St FinBarr', painted in 1831 (one of two versions) attempts to put the viewer in the heart of the Shehy Mountains. There is a sense of nostalgia to this work, the search for a lost past. Petrie's Gougane Barra captures a moment — depicting a magnificent sky, shifting clouds, a veil of mist and a beam of sunlight breaking through. The light falls perpendicular as if from heaven, lighting up and highlighting the ruins of the old Christian pilgrimage island, part of Ireland's cultural identity. The meeting of the sky, the Shehy Mountains, the lonely lake and the shoreline of the lake are seen clearly, all contrasting with the small human figures shown in the foreground. There are dark colours, which convey a feeling of eeriness, a wilderness and a powerful landscape carved out and protected by nature. There is intense emotion on the painter's behalf. (Image 13 in colour section).

1.5 The Candle in the Dark — the Tailor and Ansty

The Shehy Mountains make different impressions on people: in 1941 one visitor — Eric Cross — was enthralled by the vistas of Gougane and the lives of its people. He wrote a series of articles in *The Bell* about two larger-than-life residents of Gougane: the Tailor, Tim Buckley, and his wife Ansty, Anastasia. Eric Cross was born in Newry, County Down, in 1905 and was educated as a chemical engineer. He came across the Tailor and Ansty while on a holiday to west Cork in the late 1930s and early 1940s. His interest in human nature led him to come back to Gougane on several occasions and to interview the Tailor at length about his life.

In 1964, Eric Cross compiled and published a series of articles on the Tailor. Eric chose Cork writer Frank O'Connor, another lover of all that Gougane has to offer, to write the introduction. It is clear from Eric Cross' work that he was attempting to describe a couple who symbolized the magic and culture of rural Ireland — and maybe indirectly explain to us today why so many Cork people, Irish people and foreigners, flock to or retreat to the sanctuary for holidays in West Cork.:

The Tailor and Ansty, *c.*1940 (Source: Eric Cross collection).

I was not alone in this thraldom to the old couple of Garrynapeaka. The Tailor's fireside was the gathering place for a host of friends, whenever they could manage it, not only from Ireland but also from England and America. It was as a memoir for these many friends that I originally wrote The Tailor and Ansty…*It was then serialised in Sean O'Faolain's periodical,* The Bell. *Later it was published in book form by the highly respectable publishers, Chapman and Hall. The publication roused the rancour of that small but active body of Pharisees, which exist in every country, driving them to ugly words and deeds and the banning of the book. The banning gave rise to a public controversy, which eventually brought about the book's 'unbanning'.*

Life could be, and was, lived with an enormous appetite, gusto, gaiety, courage, and a certainty, which made hay of the various religious, philosophical and political labels with which we buttressed ourselves against the real in our individual lives. We were, in fact, privileged to participate in the lives of two people, near to the end of their lives, who had preserved still the innocence, the zest, the wonder and the faults of children. That Johnny Con's cow had had a black calf; that Patsy Dan had received a letter that morning; that Hitler had invaded Russia, were all occasions for 'Well, Glory be. Now that for 'oo!' from Ansty. A hen crossing the road; the mislaying of his hat; the marvellous fact of waking up in the morning were, to the Tailor, all great and marvellous events, worthy of consideration and comment. 'Come day. Go day. God send another day.' 'Take the world fine and aisy and the world will take you fine and aisy.' "The world is only a blue-bag. Knock a squeeze out of it when you can.' 'Imagination was given us not to make the worst of a good job. Any fool can do that. It was given us to make the best of a bad job.' The life of Garrynapeaka was lived on these terms. A candle shining through the dark. [4]

4. Eric Cross, 1941, *The Tailor and Ansty*, (Mercier Press, Cork) p.25.

Seán O'Faoláin in later years (O'Faoláin collection, Cork City Library)

1.6 The Free Country, the Unfree City

Frank O'Connor, Daniel Corkey and Seán Ó Faoláin are just three eminent Cork sons whose biographical works also touch on the magic of the early stages of the River Lee Valley. Cork writer Seán Ó Faolain (1900-1991) in his autobiography *Vive Moi!* describes some of the magic of his youth in West Cork.

Of all our expeditions the most favoured by Eileen and by me was to the source of the Lee, beyond the small leaden lake of Gougane Barra, which is backed by a long, dark, dead end valley or coom, known in Irish as Coom Ruadh, *or the Red Coom, in English as Valley Desmond. All our symbols were concentrated in this glen…We loved this valley, lake, ruined chapel and rude cloister because of their enclosure, their memories, and their silence. Many times then and in after years we entered the silent dead end coom to climb the mountain beyond. Once we got lost there in a summer fog, aiming for the minute loch up there called the Lake of the Speckled Trout, dark as ink and cold as ice water, visited otherwise only by mountain sheep.*

When we reached the top of the coom, after some tough climbing, the fog lifted and we came on another valley, and a vast view westward across other mountain tips far over the sunset sea. On those fortresses what could touch us? We enjoyed among them what I may well call a juvenile fantasy of grown desire, planning tiny cottages on either side of this lost valley or that, facing one another, so that by day we would descend to the lake and be together there and by night see, each, the other's beckoning light across the darkness of the glen [5].

5. O'Faoláin, S., 1963, *Vive Moi!*, (Sinclair-Stevenson Press, London) p.52.

II

FURTHER FOOTSTEPS —
TRANSFORMATIONS IN THE RIVER VALLEY

2.1 *In the Heart of Uíbh Laoghaire*

A little to the east of the island [Gougane] is the exit of the Lee. Its shallow bed is here crossed by a few stepping stones, shortly below which the stream is heard sounding wildly, and its course seen impeded by rude masses of naked rock, standing out stubbornly, as if in resistance to its escape, or forming rough and irregular ledges, over which it is hurried, bounding deliriously from rock, to rock, and sweeping with headlong rapidity, chafed and all in foam. [6]

Uíbh Laoghaire, or (in its English derivative) Iveleary, means 'the descendants of Laoghaire' and is applied to the territory which they inhabited. Before the Anglo-Norman invasion of Ireland (from 1169 onwards) there were four great divisions in County Cork. One of those divisions was Muscraidhe (Muskerry), in the north of the county. Muskerry, or Musc Raighe, means 'the territory of Cairbre Musc'. Cairbre Musc were a family of Celts who lived in the area in the third century AD. Muscraidhe was sub-divided into three parts, one of which was called Muscraidhe Uí Fhloinn, now the barony of West Muskerry, which contains fifteen parishes and extends to the borders of Kerry. As the name indicates, the O'Flynns were the early lords of this territory, but its history is mainly associated with the MacCarthys.

O'Leary country, formerly known as Tuath Ruis, was in the south of Cork in a part of the present diocese of Ross. Shortly after the Anglo-Norman Invasion, the O'Learys were driven into the western part of Muscraidhe Uí Fhloinn and the district became known as Uíbh Laoghaire. Uíbh Laoghaire is now understood to encompass the district and the parish of Inchigeela in the west of Cork. It may be said to comprise the basin of the Lee from its source at Gougane Barra to halfway between the village of Inchigeela and the town of Macroom. The Lee runs from west to east through the district, and by far the greater part of Uíbh Laoghaire lies to the north of the river; the two chief villages being Inchigeela and Ballingeary.

What strikes a visitor most on coming to the district is the absence of forests. In ancient times, the Lee Valley had extensive forests but throughout the centuries clearances to provide agricultural land reduced them considerably. English plantations in the mid- to late sixteenth century were responsible for substantial clearance. Charles Smith, writing his *History of Cork* in 1750, remarked on the area:

---

6. Windele, J., 1846, *Guide to the South of Ireland*, (Messrs. Bolster, Cork) p. 293.

Rossalougha Clapper Bridge, near the exit of the River Lee from Gougane Barra Lake (picture: K. McCarthy).

About 100 years ago this country was all a forest. The woods consisted of large oak, birch, alder, some ash, and many yews, of as great bulk as the largest oak. Great quantities of fir are still taken out of the turf bogs. This forest was then stored with red and fallow deer, and abounded with great ayries of excellent hawks, which, with the timber, belonged to the Earl of Cork. [7]

The former abundance of timber is evident in the place names. Doire, an oakwood, with its derivatives Doirín and Daireach, is used either by itself or in compound names of many places in this district. Hence there is Doirín na nGlas (Derreenglass), Derreen near Inchigeela, Doirín Donaidhe near Keimaneigh, Daireach between Ballingeary and Ballyvourney, Leacan-a-daraighe near Ceim an Fhia, Doirín a Buarca, Doirin Aonaigh, Doire Bhán, Doire Rioghbhardain, and several others. From Ros, a wood, come Ros a Locha at Gougane, Ros Mór near Inchigeela, and Each-Ros, north of Ballingeary. Other place names that highlight the natural history of this district are Céim an Fhia, 'the pass of the deer' and Nadanuller, a hill at Gougane, meaning 'the eagle's nest'. In recent decades, a reforestation programme has enhanced the region further. It was acquired in 1938 by the Irish government's forestry department Coilte, who gradually reforested the region over several decades. They largely planted lodgepole pine, Sitka spruce and Japanese larch. Over 20,000 acres have been replanted in the Lee catchment area. Gougane Barra forest park accounts for some 3,163 acres.

7. Smith, C. *A History of Cork* (Cork), p.189.

The parish of Inchigeela comprises more than 45,000 English acres. The parish is divided into 120 townlands, which vary much in size. Eleven of these townlands are in the barony of East Carbery while the remainder lie in West Muskerry. When Samuel Lewis published his Topographical Dictionary of Ireland in 1837, the population of Inchigeela parish was 5,783, while the population in the 1911 census was 3,242. In 1837, the parish comprised:

A total of 2,000 acres of woodland, 130 common, 2,500 arable, 12,000 pasture, 7,000 bog, and the remainder waste. The surface is mountainous, rocky, and of wild aspect, but towards the east more level and in a state of profitable cultivation; the chief manure used by farmers of the eastern portion is lime brought from Anaghely, near Macroom, and by those of the western portion, a calcareous coral sand from Bantry Bay... There is a day-school under the superintendence of the rector, who contributes to its support; the house is rent-free. There are four National school-houses in the parish; three were erected by the R.C. clergyman and his parishioners, one at Kilbarry, one at Inchigeelagh, and one at Ballingearig; the fourth was built at Coolmountain in 1836 in aid of which the Commissioners of Education who granted £30...The average attendance of children, both male and female, at these four schools is 500. [8]

2.2 *Manoeuvres in Keimaneigh*

The Pass of Keimaneigh is a wild and rugged boundary between the coastal region of Bantry Bay in west Cork and the mountainous terrain that encompasses areas like Gougane Barra and the upper River Lee Valley. Over three kilometres long, the pass originated as a meltwater channel from a melting glacier 20,000 years ago. There are sheer cliffs rising each side to a height of 100 feet above the road. Today the pass marks the official division between the small Irish-speaking area of the West Cork Gaeltacht and the rest of the region. In the past, it was the dividing line between the Gaelic Irish families of the O'Sullivans and O'Learys.

The mountain pass is immortalised by local poet Máire Bhuí Ní Laoire in her poem 'Cath Céim An Fhia', an account of a battle in 1822 between local Whiteboys and yeomen supported by British soldiers. A memorial in the middle of the pass recalls the conflict. It was economics, not politics that determined the tragic events. The Irish tenant farmer and the labourer experienced much economic hardship in 1810 and the 1820s. A change in the political system, nearly 180 years previously (in the 1640s), had meant that many Irish landlords who chose not to be loyal to the English government had their lands dispossessed and handed over to English gentry. The landlord system that was put into place strengthened and evolved in the eighteenth century and brought with it rent increases for tenants and evictions for non-payment of rent.

Among the many resistance movements and secret societies established across Ireland were the Whiteboys, who operated at night carrying out raids against their persecutors. After the Napoleonic Wars ended in 1815, a downturn in the economy caused a serious depression across the British Empire. West Cork was severely hit by the near-end of the lucrative trade of supplying ships with butter and other provisions in Cork harbour.

By 1822 the methods used by the secret societies were also changing. The Whiteboys had operated in bands of twenty to thirty, coming out at night and returning to their homes before dawn. The new secret societies were now forming large encampments up in the hills and staying there for long periods. They were better organised. The local historical record of Iveleary for January 1822 recalls that the Keimaneigh area was used as a base for random

8. Lewis, S., 1837, *Topographical Dictionary of Ireland* (Dublin), p.257.

Pass of Keimaneigh Memorial (picture: K. McCarthy).

attacks meant to express condemnation of rent oppression. Local folklore calls those men who gathered in the pass Rockites, rather than Whiteboys. The gathering in Keimaneigh was not unique and similar large groups of men were operating all over West Cork and elsewhere. One report of the time suggests that there were two thousand men at Keimaneigh and five thousand in the camps that lay between Macroom and Millstreet. Those numbers are probably exaggerated, but the bands were obviously large.

The first incident in Keimaneigh took place during the night of Friday 11 January 1822 when a party of about five hundred Rockites raided a number of homes of the gentry in the Bantry area looking for weapons. They had some success, acquiring a number of muskets but no ammunition. The reaction by the gentry was instant and aggressive. The following day, Saturday 12 January, Lord Bantry and his brother Captain White assembled a party of about fifty yeomanry and rode out in pursuit of the Rockites. The yeomanry were uniformed, mounted on horse and armed with sabres and pistols. Riding through the pass they came upon the Rockites near Ballingeary, who rushed up into the hills and made their way back to the pass on foot. Realising how dangerous their position was, the yeomanry retreated back through the pass, avoiding the stones that were hurled down from the heights. They then rode back to Bantry without having achieved anything.

The authorities in Bantry were not going to let matters rest there. They organized another war party, which set out at 5a.m. on Monday 21 January 1822. The Rockites numbered about four hundred and were mostly armed with spades or pitchforks, about fourteen muskets — some very ancient — and little or no ammunition. The ensuing battle lasted all day. The mounted yeomanry rode down towards Inchigeelagh and took a few captives before turning back to rejoin the soldiers. The Rockites took shelter where they could until the soldiers had fired all their ammunition, and some sporadic hand-to-hand fighting took place.

Eventually the Rockites returned to their superior position above the pass and prepared to dislodge a few large rocks so they would land on the war party. Most of the yeomanry

Pass of Keimaneigh on Bantry — Macroom R584 Road (picture: K. McCarthy).

Pass of Keimaneigh (picture: K. McCarthy).

scrambled through the pass before the falling stones blocked it. A large foot party had to return by the old Bantry road, adding about thirty kilometres to their march. In the evening the war party returned to Bantry leaving the Rockites in possession of the pass and controlling all movement through.

Towards the end of January 1822 a party of Rockites burned down Kilbarry House, the home of local landlord James Barry in the night. The Barry family had built their mansion from the stones of an old O'Leary tower house, Carrignaneelagh Castle, in the eastern end of Uíbh Laoghaire parish. After the burning Barry summoned all his tenants and made them pull down the old castle and use the stone to rebuild his house. Kilbarry House still stands today. Barry must have persuaded the authorities in Dublin that his part in the skirmish was very important, because he was amply rewarded for his contribution and the losses he suffered.

In early February 1822 the Rockites abandoned their encampment in Keimaneigh and returned to their homes and farms. According to local records, many members of the group realised that they had made their protest and that there was not much more they could do. Their decisions may have been influenced by thoughts of reprisals, which did follow. Lord Wellesley, the Lord Lieutenant in Cork City, set up a special commission to try the large number of prisoners taken at several affrays in Carriganimma, Deshure, Newmarket and at Keimaneigh. Altogether, thirty-six men were sentenced to be hanged. In addition, it was most likely cold and wet in the winter of 1822 and there would have been a shortage of food. Local lore suggests that the actual number of Rockites killed was anything up to twelve people.

2.3 *Unravelling Ballingeary*

'All human landscape is an unwitting autobiography, reflecting our tastes, our values, our aspiration and even our fears, in a tangible and visible form.' [9]

The landscape of the early stages of the River Lee in west Cork provides an opportunity to discuss how old and modern Ireland can be seen to be embodied by the landscape in ways that often conflict. There is, for example, the plight of a warring Gaelic Irish family like the O'Learys who tried to keep their lands from the English colonizer over eight hundred years ago to the Battle of Keimaneigh in 1822, and then there is what the Gaeltacht region of today means to people. Seán Ó Suilleabháin, the Chairman of the Ballingeary Historical Society notes: 'the history of a place is a continuous and evolving process…in a place such as Uíbh Laoghaire, there is a very long line of memory; today's events are as important as the past.'

The *Discovery Series* Ordnance Survey map of the landscape shows some insights into the history of the Ballingeary area but this is very much a place that must be traversed and seen to be understood. Inchinossig Bridge is the first bridge that the river flows under on its journey to Cork harbour. Inchinossig, or *Inse an Fhosaigh*, means 'level spot of the encampment'. The name is based on local folklore claiming that the area was once used as a staging point of attack or attacks. It is not known what period of time or who the name refers to. Whatever the case, there was possibly a causeway that provided a crossing.

Crossing points of rivers usually create associated settlements. Further downstream lies Dromanallig Clapper Bridge, a stone causeway that looks quite old and predates the

9. Meinig, D.W. (Ed.), 1979, *The Interpretation of Ordinary Landscapes, Geographical Landscapes* (Oxford University Press, Oxford) p.12.

Ballingeary crossroads
(picture K. McCarthy).

Inchinossig structure. It comprises thirty-two slabs of various sizes supported by stone piers. In 1987, when the river was deepened upstream, a number of slabs collapsed. Today fourteen original slabs remain in situ. The present-day Inchinossig Bridge dates to the 1820s and was probably part of a general scheme of developments that took place across Ireland at the time. Bunsheelin Bridge in Ballingeary village also dates to this time. Substantial Westminster funding was invested in the 1820s in imperial infrastructure such as new roads, bridges and architecture. The funding was dispersed through all parts of the empire by the decisions of local grand juries that comprised local landlords and magistrates.

Ballingeary village — or Béal Átha an Ghaorthaidh, 'ford mouth of the wooded glen' — is located partly in the townland of Kilmore — Choill Mhór, meaning 'large wood' — and partly in Dromanallig — Drom An AllighF, 'ridge of the rocky place'. The village is divided by the River Bunsheelin, which joins the Lee just to the east of the village. The traces of human settlement in Ballingeary provide strong evidence of change, and of the priorities of its population in the past, present and future. Many traces are concrete as well as symbolic and appear in architectural forms. Every building is colourful and many of the village's buildings date from the mid- to late twentieth century, with PVC windows prevalent throughout the settlement.

The buildings in Ballingeary seem spread out like jigsaw pieces waiting to be put together. Many buildings are detached from neighbouring buildings and back gardens. One cannot

Dromanallig Clapper Bridge, Ballingeary, Co. Cork (picture: K. McCarthy).

Inchinossig Bridge, Ballingeary (picture: K. McCarthy).

Colaiste na Mumhan, Ballingeary (est.1904) (picture: K. McCarthy).

avoid sensing the wilderness, nor can one ignore the sounds of rural Ireland while walking through the village, especially with the Shehy Mountains looming over the settlement. The importance of preserving cultural stability through the village's Gaeltacht status and especially through the Irish College at the western end and craft shops at the eastern end of the settlement is emphasized here. One also gets the impression that parts of the village, such as its old cabins, old schools and an old church site, have not only been worn down by time and forgotten but perhaps more importantly they have been left to decay because of the need to focus on sustainable development in Ballingeary.

Every town has public spaces of importance, sites that the local population have chosen for the visitor to note. In Ballingeary a number of monuments across the village remind visitors of Irish nationalism, nationhood, social chaos and cultural revival in the nineteenth and twentieth centuries. The sites highlighted tend to make observers reminisce about a 'lost Ireland', a past more important to some than the present or future.

At the eastern entrance to the village stands Coláiste na Mumhan, which was opened on 4 July 1904 to help young students learn Irish. Over one hundred years later, this college successfully plays host to over four hundred students who converge on Ballingeary every summer. On its walls facing the road is a plaque with the names of past supporters of the college. It notes their role in the Irish War of Independence and includes patriots Tomas MacCurtain and Terence MacSwiney.

Directly across the road from Coláiste na Mumhan we find Terence MacSwiney GAA Park. Born in 1879 in Cork City, MacSwiney was educated in North Monastery CBS and developed a keen interest in Irish literature at a young age. He obtained a degree in philosophy from the Royal University of Dublin. At the age of fifteen he became a trainee accountant at the office of Dwyer & Co. and stayed there for seventeen years. He joined the Gaelic League in Cork, was active in the Irish Volunteers and devoted much time to literary and dramatic groups like the Young Ireland Society and the Celtic Literary Society. Between 1910 and 1914 MacSwiney wrote five plays, two of which were in verse. One of his greatest works, *Principles of Freedom*, appeared in serial form in the Dublin monthly paper *Irish Freedom*. The entire work was published in New York in 1921.

In 1916 in anticipation of the Easter Rising, Terence MacSwiney and Tomás MacCurtain mobilised local volunteers, but their efforts were in vain: the Cork contingent never made it to Dublin because of communication problems. However, MacSwiney was arrested for his involvement in the attempt and was released six months later, when he reorganised the Volunteers in Cork. He received enormous support after MacCurtain's death. He was re-arrested and transported to Brixton Prison, where he died on 25 October 1920 after a seventy-four day hunger strike.

Further along the eastern road into Ballingeary village lies the famine pot. After the Great Famine of the mid-1800s, the population of the parish of Iveleary decreased by more than a quarter. The population in 1841 was 6,357, with 1,032 cabins. By 1851, 231 cabins had been vacated and the population stood at 4,584. A soup kitchen was established in the nearby townland of Coolmountain House through the efforts of a relief committee headed up by parish priest Fr Jeremiah Holland, Rev. Sadleir and the occupier of the house and associated farm, Denis O'Leary. The famine pot is a reminder of those dark days in rural Ireland.

At the entrance to the western side of the village lies Casadh na Spríde, a man-made garden built in 1998 and dedicated to the memory of the O'Sullivan clan, who retreated here from

Ballingeary famine pot
(picture: K. McCarthy).

Cosadh na Spride, July 2006, Féile na Prataé Nua, Community Public Picnic (picture: K. McCarthy).

their winter battle with the English on the Beara Pennisula in the winter of 1601. On New Year's Eve 1602 Donal O'Sullivan Beara and his 1000 followers passed through Ballingeary on their celebrated forced retreat from their home on the Beara Peninsula to County Leitrim. They camped at Teampaillín Eachrois, a ruined church two miles north of Ballingeary. At the end of their two week ordeal only thirty-five reached their destination in O'Rourke's castle in Leitrim Village. The central interpretative plaque in Cosadh na Spride notes that the garden was made using local timber and features native flowers and plants.

At this side of the village there are also a number of craft shops, funded by Údarás na Gaeltachta. Shops selling 'quality Irish crafts and gifts' are abundant but during my visit in April 2006 they were all closed. Paddy Quill's shop awaits the summer tourist. Life in Ballingeary is very much seasonal. Ballingeary's economy of one hundred years ago was also seasonal. According to Guy's *Directory of County Cork* there were two hotels in the Ballingeary area in 1906 (James Cronin's in Gougane Barra and John Shorten in Ballingeary), one card and tucking mills (Mrs Murphy being the proprietor) and nine shops. There were five general shops with a boot maker (Michael Dromey), Mahony Corns, J. Twohig, the grocer and Michael Hyde, the butter buyer. There were seventy-six landowners noted in Ballingeary electoral divisions, many of whom probably grew and sold crops on a seasonal basis. The sizes

SS Finbarre's and Ronan's Church, Ballingeary (picture: K. McCarthy).

of their families are not noted. Today, there are at least 5,000 people in the Ballingeary area, a number that is increasing as farmers sell off land for housing, especially in the village area and on the roads along Lough Allua that link Ballingeary to Inchigeela.

In 1906 there was a fowl and butter market in Ballingeary every Tuesday. Butter firkins that were to be taken to the Cork market had to be taken by horse. Three in all could fit on a horse's back if the baskets were across the saddle. It would take a night to go to Cork to be there when the market opened in the morning. A farmer could spend a day at the market and a night coming home. So all in all, it was a long journey compared to the hour and a quarter spent travelling by car to Ballingeary today. In addition, in 1906 the nearest telegraph, post and money order offices were in Inchigeela, with the nearest constabulary barracks in Macroom.

Parish churches act as a village cross or as the village fountain, where residents meet to pray, to celebrate their faith and community, and afterwards to discuss the needs of the community informally. SS Finbarre and Ronan's Church in the centre of Ballingeary stands on a raised sandstone platform, a sign of its importance in the community. In the churchyard the church bell can be seen in a concrete tower with a rope hanging to the ground. In the same churchyard there is an elaborate sculpture of St Finbarre, completed by Cork sculptor Seamus O'Murchada. It is evidence that people still believe in the myth of Finbarre, and that for the local population religion continues to be a source of inspiration. The statue sits on a pedestal inscribed with the words, 'In memory of the exiles of Ireland', perhaps referring to emigration or even the flight of the Irish earls in the aftermath of the Battle of Kinsale in 1601.

In the eighteenth century, the old Roman Catholic church stood at the south-western end of the village. Mass was said in the church every other Sunday, so parishioners would have to travel to Inchigeela on alternate Sundays. In the early years of the 1800s, Fr Jeremiah Holland raised funds to build a new church on the present-day site. Originally built in 1809, the site was provided rent-free by Mr Graham, the local landlord. Flagstones and slate for the church were obtained at a local quarry at Illauninagh. In 1831 Fr Holland also organized funding and support to build a school at the south-east angle of the present-day chapel yard.

By 1859 the congregation had grown in numbers and decided to extend the building. The eastern wall was broken down and the modern nave was constructed. The old door and window were closed up and the present-day doors at the north and south sides respectively were created. The altar was changed around to face the new nave. A new gallery was erected at the east end, the back of the new church nave. In 1888 Fr Hurley decided to make further improvements, so two new sacristies were built, and new stained glass windows were inserted along with new seats, roofs and a ceiling. Porches and a baptistery were also constructed. Sarah Sutherland gave a gift in 1889 of the elaborate stained glass window of St Finbarre that is there today. A plaque nearby commemorates Eugene Moynihan, a Ballingeary man who emigrated to America and died there in 1925.

Apart from the things one would normally expect in a church, like the baptismal fonts and side altars and the image of St Finbarre, there is also a stained glass window depicting St Ronan, drawn by Padraig O'Ronan. The Ronan family owned the local corn mill in Ballingeary for many years. It is not known whether Ballingeary's St Ronan is directly connected with the owners of the mills or if St Ronan is a character chosen to symbolise the character of the local community.

There are twelve Irish saints bearing the name of Ronan. The one celebrated in the window is St Ronan of Iona, who St Bede refers to as one of those who defended the Roman way of calculating Easter rather than the Celtic way. At the Synod of Whitby in 664 St Ronan's ideas were upheld. This St Ronan has his feast day on 7 February and is commemorated by St Ronan's Well at Innerleithen in Peeblesshire where, according to tradition, the saint came to the valley and drove out the devil. The saint is usually depicted squashing a serpent as is the case with the stained glass window in Ballingeary church. A similar image can be seen in Gougane Barra oratory — hence the link between the two saints.

2.4 *Wonders of Lough Allua and Oileán Uí Mhaothagáin*

A small mile west of Inchigeela, the River Lee opens into a fine lake, called Lough Allua, three English miles long, and a half mile broad, stretching out into several bays; it is deep, and not fordable from end to end. Salmon trouts, almost as large as salmon, small river trout of various kinds, and eels abound in it; also the charr or Alpine Trout. [10]

Lough Allua on any day is beautiful to behold and is such a contrast to the overwhelming Shehy Mountains in the distance. One now gets a feeling for the river's movement and journey towards its mouth, especially because of its growing strength. Lough Allua, between Ballingeary and Inchigeela in West Cork, provokes many emotions in the visitor. In spite of the encroaching 'bungalow blitz' culture along the shoreline of the lake, Lough Allua seems carved into the local geology. The surrounding landscape conveys all kinds of messages to the visitor but not in an obvious way. To get a feel for Lough Allua, you have to circumnavigate it or boat across it. The topography of Lough Allua has that sense of wilderness, with enjoyable scenery for the visitor and for the modern bungalow owner, all of which contrasts with the habitats of local wildlife and fowl.

10. Smith, C. *A History of Cork* (Cork) p.190.

Horatio Townsend tells us in his *General and Statistical Survey of the County of Cork* that in the 1700s there was large-scale destruction of timber in the area. He observes of Lough Allua:

The native beauty of these lakes has been much impaired by the loss of their timber, which even the solitary remoteness of their situation has not been able to preserve from the hand of the destroyer. Thirty years ago they might have almost vied, upon a smaller scale, with the rich scenery of Killarney itself. Besides the woodlands, which skirted the lake, the little islands of which Inchigeelagh has several, were then adorned with trees and shrubs. Of all this variety of sylvan decoration scarce a vestige is now remaining [11]

The cutting down of timber is not the first indication of change in the landscape. There is evidence that there were settlements in the lake area as early as the Bronze Age (*circa* 2,500 BC). Here on the northern side of Lough Allua, in the townland of Currahy, a standing stone and a stone row stand as markers from communities dating back to the later part of prehistory. The standing stone is located on the shoreline of the lake, perhaps symbolising the control and power of its Bronze Age residents over the area.

A clump of trees in Lough Allua is evidence of an early medieval settlement (*circa* 800 AD) in the form of a crannóg. A crannóg, 'a small island built with young trees', is an artificial circular or oval island constructed in a lake. In general, they were built with dumped layers of brushwood, timbers, stone, soil and peat. A palisade or fence encompassed many sites. Access to crannógs was over stepping-stones, by bridge or boat. In general, they were built in an area of shallow water within easy reach of the shore.

There are at least 1,200 known crannóg sites in Ireland, mostly in small lakelands in the north-west and north-east. However, these happen to be locations where specialist Irish archaeologists have concentrated their research, so there may be many more crannóg sites waiting to be recognised. Scientific tree ring dating in Antrim, Fermanagh and Down reveals that the building of crannóg began in early medieval times (500 AD-1200 AD) and continued in use at least into the 1600s.

Many crannóg sites today survive as small tree-clad islands in lakes and bear little resemblance to the original crannógs. This is the case with Lough Allua. It is the only known site in Cork and one of over a dozen known sites in Munster. It is not known why it was built but it can at least be speculated that there was political instability in Ireland at some stage in early Christian Ireland, which made communities anxious to defend themselves. A crannóg would have been highly visible and difficult to construct in wetland conditions. Crannóg size would have started small and then have been elaborated on as time went on.

A range of social classes from local lords to craftsmen would have occupied crannógs. Several crannóg sites that have been excavated in Ireland have revealed themselves to be royal residences, craft centres, refuges from raiding parties, places to store objects, seasonal spaces to live — some may even be artificial mounds that marked territory or routeways. Waterlogged conditions meant that rich archaeological deposits are preserved, including wooden houses, palisades and pathways, thousands of metal, glass, wooden, bone and leather artefacts, plant remains, seeds, beetles and animal bone. Archaeological and historical evidence suggests that several Irish crannógs were in use for very long periods of time before they were destroyed or abandoned.

The Lough Allua crannóg is called Oileán Uí Mhaothagáin (Mehigan's Island). Legend has it that Mhaothagáin was a Gaelic Irish chieftain of O'Leary descent. Others say that it should be *Meathain*, which in English means twigs and saplings. The word Meathain appears in an adjacent townland name: Doire an Mheathain (Derryvane). The nearby lakeside shore is 200

11. Townsend, H., 1815, *General and Statistical Survey of the County of Cork* (Edwards and Savage, Cork) p.118.

Scenic Lough Allua (picture: K. McCarthy).

feet above sea level and slopes gently to the lakeshore. Crannógs were located next to good land for cattle and sheep pasture. Lough Allua is not too windswept or stormy and is sheltered by the fertile sides of the Lee basin.

Oileán Uí Mhaothagáin is a typical lake settlement and is home to ten to twelve sally trees and some rushes and reeds. During the wet weather, the crannóg is covered with water. It is located in a little cove on the northern shore of Lough Allua, nearly one metre above the water level and built on a stone platform. On her visit to the island local woman Máire Uí Léime noted:

The crannóg it is roughly circular in shape (c.10m by 13m), it is very uneven under foot — trees have twisted downwards and re-rooted in the ground and a lot of the roots can be seen twisting around the stones, some clays, tree roots and stones litter the ground underfoot with no physical remains of the ancient site.

Apart from the crannóg, the surrounding townland names reflect human presence over time. For the townlands to be given names, people had to be present; something had to have had happened. The various names remind the visitor of the layout of the land and its

Lough Allua crannóg (picture: K. McCarthy).

Lough Allua crannóg reconstruction (source: O'Sullivan, 2000).

Left: Lough Allua standing stone in Currahy townland with local resident and Chairman of Ballingeary Historical Society, Seán Ó Súlleabháin (picture: K. McCarthy).

Below: Lough Allua Mass rock in Curraheen townland (picture: K. McCarthy).

closeness to nature. At Kilmore, or *Coill Mhór*, at the north side of the Lough, there is an old graveyard named *Cillín Leasa Ronáin*, meaning 'little fort church of St Ronáin'. Other place names include: Turnaspidogy or *Tír na Spideoige*, meaning 'district of the robin'; Illauninagh East and Illauniagh West, or *Oileán Aibhneach*, meaning 'islands formed by the river'; Keavaugh Beg or *Caol-Mhagh*, meaning 'narrow plane', or *Caolbhach*, meaning 'place of the saplings' or light plantation'; Inchideraille or *Inse Idir Dhá Fhaill*, meaning 'river inch between two rocks', Gortnarea or *Gort na Reidhe*, meaning 'field of the moorland'; Coornahahilly or *Cuar na Haith-Thuile*, meaning 'corner of the occasional flooding'; Gortaknockane or *Gort a'Chnocain*, meaning 'field of the hillock'; Cooragreenane or *Cuar a'Ghrianáin* or 'sunny hill-back'; Curaheen or *Curraichán*, meaning 'little swamp' and Cappanaclare or *Ceapach an Chláir*, meaning 'clearance of the flat land'.

Much of the history of this place has been forgotten, but the Lough remains constant. The presence of standing stones, a crannóg and even a mass rock are evidence of centuries of people living, working and even praying by Lough Allua.

2.5 *Inchigeela Narratives*

The Lee emerges at the eastern end of Lough Allua and continues on its journey. Next up is Inchigeelagh, the unofficial capital of the parish of Uíbh Laoghaire that straddles the River Lee. It is said to have gotten its name from its Irish derivative *Inse Geimhleach* or 'the island of the hostages'. Local folklore tells of an incident several centuries ago when the O'Learys took some Danes hostage on the island that is now the River Island Amenity Park. The Danes were called Macoitir and their descendants today are the Cotters. The O'Leary family name is still common in Inchigeela. It is O'Leary homeland — the family is connected and rooted to the place. Today the O'Learys are sub-divided into septs across the world. Every year, local men Peter O'Leary, Joe Creedon and Eugene O'Leary organise an annual O'Leary Clan Gathering, where members come from the four corners of the world to celebrate the family's heritage. Exploring the main village graveyard, which was opened in 1925, one can find the names of numerous other families who have also shaped the life of Inchigeela, like the O'Sullivans, Moynihans, McCarthys, O'Sheas, Murphys, Lyons, Creedons, Creeds, Luceys, O'Callaghans, Mannings, Kellehers, Buckleys, Healys and Oldhams.

The early historic record for Inchigeelagh is limited. A local standing stone (now missing) marked on the Ordnance Survey in Carrigleigh or *Carrig Liath*, meaning 'grey rock', reminds us that there were people living in the area in the Bronze Age (*circa* 2,500 BC). The local tower house in Carrignacurra, built by the O'Learys, records the defence of their territory in the fifteenth century AD Fast forward to 1750 when Charles Smith in his *A History of Cork* describes an English barracks and the attraction of a gold-like substance in the river:

Inshigeelagh, six miles S.W. of Macroom, has a good barrack for one foot company, built in a stone fort of four bastions, erected on the north end of a bridge over the Lee. Near this place, many pieces of a metallic substance have been found, in the form of cubes, as hard as iron, and glittering with sparks, intermixed, of a pale yellow, shining like gold. These cubes are washed out of the rocks on the banks of the river by winter floods. [12]

In 1837 Samuel Lewis, in his *Topographical Dictionary of Ireland*, describes further change and continuity in the area, noting:

---

12. Smith, C. A History of Cork (Cork) p.190.

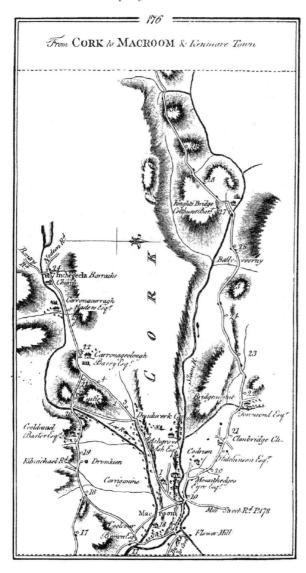

Taylor and Skinner's *Road Map* of
Inchigeela, Co. Cork, 1779 (source:
Cork City Library).

*The surface is mountainous, rocky, and of wild aspect, but towards the east more level and in a state
of profitable cultivation; the chief manure used by farmers of the eastern portion is lime brought from
Anaghely near Macroom, and by those of the western portion, a calcareous coral from Bantry Bay. The
principal seats are Boyle Grove, the residence of J. Boyle, Lee Mount of J. Barter, Kilbarry, the glebe-
house of the Rev. Dr Baldwin; and the cottage, of the Rev. J. Holland. In the village [Inchigeela] is a
constabulary police station, and fairs are held on May 31st, Aug. 31st, and Dec. 3rd, horses, cattle, sheep, and
pigs; these fairs were very numerous and well attended, but have grown almost into disuse.* [13]

The vibrancy of present-day Inchigeela is based on characters who have come to or passed
through Inchigeela. This area of West Cork appears in the works of Cork literary giants like Daniel
Corkery, Frank O'Connor, Seán Ó Faolain and revolutionary Terence McSwiney. The place has

---

13. Lewis, S., 1837, *Topographical Dictionary of Ireland*, (Dublin) p.258.

Portrait of Inchigeela (artist: Don Holland).

Creedon's Hotel (picture: K. McCarthy).

Left: Portrait of Joe Creedon,
Creedon's Hotel, Inchigeela
(picture: Laurence Hudson).

Below: Inchigeela, *c.*1900
(picture: Creedon's Hotel).

Life and death, Inchigeela, (picture: K. McCarthy).

been an inspiration for revolution and a kind of an entrance in Daniel Corkery's own words to a 'Hidden Ireland'. Today, there still is affection for Inchigeela, which has become a sort of 'cultural capital' of West Cork. An old roller stands outside the Crannóg Store and Café, with 'Pride of the Lee Valley' written on it. At the entrance stand four flags, from left to right: Ireland, Cork, the EU and the USA. Perhaps the order is an indication of Inchigeela's sense of belonging.

Inchigeela is a small village with a big proud heart. It does not have any noticeable memorials — unlike Ballingeary, which has large memorials commemorating the famine and St Finbarre. Here the emphasis is on family and community. Death, faith, living and law and order are all within one hundred metres of each other. Any historical artefacts or markers displayed are straightforward, such as the two interpretive plaques in the village detailing the history of the Protestant church and society and of the village community. There is a grotto on the way to Inchigeela from Macroom that gives the visitor a sense of the community spirit in Inchigeela. Opposite the Catholic church is the St Joseph, Patron of Families House of Prayer and there are signs asking drivers to slow down because there are children crossing, all of which are signs of an active and growing community.

In the church grounds by the front gate there is a small plaque highlighting the planting of an ash tree by Bishop John Buckley, a native of Inchigeela, on the occasion of his appointment as Bishop of Cork and Ross in 1998. The largest memorial in Inchigeela is located on the grounds of the Church of St Finbarre and the Little Angels. Here there is a large high cross commemorating the contribution of the Holland family to religious life in Inchigeela and across Britain and Ireland. Fr Jeremiah Holland was parish priest of Inchigeela during the Great Famine and was responsible for the development of several schools and the Catholic churches in Ballingeary and Inchigeela. The contribution of his nephew, Rev. J. Holland, PP of Inchigeela in the mid- to late-1800s is also remembered on another side of the memorial.

Rev. John Canon Holland was parish priest of Passage and Shanbally, Cork, and died in 1858. Rev. Jeremiah C. Holland was parish priest. in the Diocese of Liverpool in the late 1800s. Other parish priests are noted in the interior of the church with one of the key stained glass windows dedicated to St Finbarre and donated by Rev. Cornelius O'Leary (parish priest from 1908-1913) and Rev. James O'Leary (parish priest from 1913-1921).

Inchigeela, like Ballingeary, has a rugged feel to it. Backgardens here are like the wilderness of the Lee Valley. Walking through the village, one finds aspects of an older and undisturbed time in Inchigeela's history, such as the tin hardware shop straddling a tributary stream of the Lee. It becomes apparent that the key changes to this settlement occurred *circa* 1820-1960, with very few 'villagescape' changes in the last four decades. Developments have also been piecemeal.

Creedon's Hotel is like the 'city hall' of Inchigeela. Its proprietor Joe Creedon is a man who is clearly proud of the history of the place. The lounge of the hotel is quaint, and the history of the Creedon family, Cork's GAA wins, the Irish War of Independence, Tom Barry and the Flying Columns and Joe's love of art are all displayed here. Joe Creedon describes Inchigeela as *'a curiosity town, an inspiring place… a beautiful woman… a muse… a world of its own…'.* Joe is one of nine brothers and four sisters. His brothers John and Conal are well known for their broadcasting and literary works respectively. Joe, like a mayor, is well-connected in his home town. He has a variety of interests: a local school heritage programme, the annual O'Leary Clan gathering, the local farmers' market and the Daniel Corkery Summer School. The summer school includes lectures, music, art exhibitions and workshops on aspects of Irish history. Joe notes that cultural tourism is not a new concept in the village and highlights the work of Bord Fáilte in the 1950s and 1960s promoting West Cork and locations such as Inchigeela.

Creedon's Hotel is perhaps one of the oldest licensed premises in County Cork, dating back to before 1800. The development of local roads by grand juries meant that Creedon's Hotel was once a coaching inn based on a main road that ran from Cork to Bantry. The Lake Hotel across the road from Creedons was established in 1810 and is also testament to the fact that there have always been people passing through the area. Francis Guy's *Directory of County Cork* in 1886 notes that the population of the parish was 4,345, with 50 landowners listed, a figure that soared to 133 by 1921. This possibly was due to children of key landowners claiming land in their adulthood, making subdivision necessary. All of these families needed access to the services of a village.

Creedon's Hotel has been revamped over time, moving from a thatched one-storey inn in the 1800s, with open fires in all rooms, to the two-storey centrally heated hotel of today. Joe reminds me on my visit that the hotel was commandeered during the War of Independence and the Irish Civil War. In 1941, Joe's great-grandfather Con Creedon and his wife Nora Cotter bought the hotel from the Corcoran family. Previous proprietors were the Brophy and the Delea families. In Guy's *Directory of County Cork* in 1921, Con Creedon was recorded as being a butter merchant, grocer and newsagent, all trades that would be at the heart of a rural village. Indeed, the number of traders listed in 1886 is half that listed in 1921, highlighting that village life was vibrant in Inchigeela in the early 1900s. The Creedon family were part of an influx of trades into the area.

Apart from the Creedons', over ten trades are listed in Guy's *Directory of County Cork* for 1921. Denis J. O'Leary was a grocer, flour and meal dealer. Listed as shopkeepers were P. Ahern, J. Corkery, Pat Cotter, Eugene Sullivan and P.J. Casey (who was also a carpenter). D. Buttimer was the boot and shoemaker. J. Corkery was listed as the car owner. The vintners were Tony Corcoran, Anne Sullivan and John McSwiney. The blacksmiths were Dennis Manning and J.Dromey (also a harness maker). Mr Manning is now remembered on a plaque near Inchigeela Bridge, which spans the River Lee. The tailors were Peter O'Leary and John O'Reilly, while J.J. Sullivan was the cycle agent and John Riordan the postman.

Walking through the village today, fewer trades are represented and the population of Inchigeela now stands at 200. However, the population will probably double soon, with twenty new houses recently finished — over thirty acres of Inchigeela's green fields have in

Ruins of Inchigeela's Church of Ireland church, which closed *c.*1885 (Picture: K. McCarthy).

recent years been rezoned for development. According to a planning permission document, seventy-two dwellings are to be built near Inchigeela's Bridge over the Lee. The possible doubling of the population will lead to a new commuter population making the village more youthful, but it will bring with it pressures for space at the local national school and a need for more community structures. In one sense, history in Inchigeela is set to repeat itself as the village reinvents itself in the twenty-first century.

2.6 Times Passes — Religion, Education and Inchigeela

This has been a place of worship for over five hundred years, and a last resting place for our loved ones — regardless of their religious convictions. Let us pray for them, and respect their memory by keeping this a place of beauty. (Interpretive plague, Inchigeela Church of Ireland ruins).

Two of the most noticeable features in Inchigeela are the Catholic church and the ruins of the Protestant church, with their respective graveyards, both of which are situated on the northern bank of the Lee. These cemeteries have served the parish of Uíbh Laoghaire for over 300 years and have been used by parishioners of all creeds. Cemeteries are often forgotten about in the study of settlements. In their silent and reflective atmosphere, the varied architectural forms of graves and tombs can reflect how old a cemetery is. Change and continuity in burial styles are indications of changing cultural and political environments. Cemeteries are markers of parochial identity, and cemetery and grave architecture reflects peoples' values and beliefs. In Inchigeela's case, the cemeteries express the relationship between the Catholic and Protestant religious communities.

Interior view of the ruins of Inchigeela's Church of Ireland church (picture: K. McCarthy).

The first reference to Inchigeela parish is in a Vatican record in 1492, the year Columbus sailed for the Americas. Local folklore notes that the church was probably in existence before the fifteenth century. The parish was and still is in the diocese of Cork. During King Henry VIII's reformation period in the mid-1500s, all parish churches were confiscated and allocated to the established Protestant Church. It took many years for this change to reach rural areas like Inchigeela, as local chieftains, the O'Learys and their followers stayed with their Catholic religion. Indeed in the visitation book of the Protestant Bishop of Cork in 1700, Dive Downes observed that there were no Protestants living within the parish and that the local Protestant church was a ruin.

In the 1690s King William of Orange and his government confiscated the lands of Uíbh Laoghaire and surrounding parishes. In June 1703, all unsold land in the region was assigned at a reduced rate to a group of London adventurers, who operated under the name of the Hollow Sword Blade Company. In 1708, the company leased the lands in the area to several new Protestant landlords. This brought more Protestant families into the community. It is unknown if they revamped the church building that Bishop Dives had seen in ruins. Decades later, in 1815, a new Protestant church was built in Inchigeela at a cost of around £230 to hold 100 people. It was financed by the Board of First Fruits, a body that had originally been set up in 1712. The Board aimed to highlight the supremacy of the 'Protestant ascendancy' over other religious groups, not just in spiritual terms but also in terms of economic and political dominance. It financially assisted the construction of churches and glebe houses throughout the country, providing plans and architects. The Board continued in operation until 1834 when the Ecclesiastical Commissioners superseded it.

Church of Holy Angels and St Finbarre, Inchigeela (picture: K. McCarthy)

A glebe house or parochial house was also built in Inchigeela in 1815, with the glebe comprising 242 and ¾ acres. In 1859, the glebe house was demolished and a new one built on the north side of the road at a cost of £647. Members of the Irish Free State Army burnt it down in 1922 to prevent it falling into the hands of the Black and Tans. That roofless two-storey ruin can be seen today as one drives into Inchigeela from the Macroom side.

In 1867 a small gabled vestry was added on the north side of the main chancel of the Church of Ireland church. At this time, a number of repairs and renovations were also carried out. After 1885, the Inchigeela Church of Ireland parish went into decay and was joined to Kilmichael and Macloneigh. All three were eventually joined to Macroom. The last resident vicar in Uíbh Laoghaire was Rev. Patrick O'Rourke, who resigned in 1885.

The shell of the nineteenth-century Protestant church has survived. Its slate roof has completely disappeared, the walls are intact and there is evidence that in recent decades, the spread of ivy across the ruin has been halted by locals with an interest in their heritage. It is a well-lit building with six large windows. Some of the window frames with iron panels have survived. One now has to imagine what it looked like with the stained glass pieces in place and the pews organised in rows in the interior. There are also timber joist holes and ledges to support a roof and wooden levels in the bell tower.

In the graveyard, there are inscribed headstones dating from the late eighteenth century to the present day. The most noticeable graves are those of wealthy merchants interred in above-ground vaults at the south-east end and include the Barrys, Boyles, Barters and Graingers. Interestingly, there are two Catholic vaults in the area for members of the O'Leary families, which shows that the communities had a pragmatic approach to one another. The most disturbing element of this area is that many of the vaults show signs of having been forced open and now reveal skeletal remains. This is obviously not the nicest of scenes to encounter when trying to unravel the history of a place.

As regards the Catholic dimension of life in Inchigeela, for nearly two centuries the Roman Catholic parish co-existed with that of the established Protestant Church. The Protestant Bishop of Cork, Dive Downes, noted in 1700 that Dennis Leary was the 'Popish' (Catholic) priest of Uíbh Laoghaire parish and Kilnamartyr in the diocese of Cloyne. He noted that he saw the walls of a church or chapel called Killbarry in the parish, two miles east of the church on the north side of the Lee.

In the early 1700s, the early years of the penal laws, Catholic worship in Inchigeela was confined to a local mass rock and another rock to the south in Kilnadur — three miles away. In November 1731, Robert Bettesworth, the then High Sheriff of County Cork and Peter Waterhouse, Bettesworth, commented on Catholic worship, stating that seven sheds were used as Mass houses by two priests and three 'Popish' schools in the marsh of Inchigeela.

In 1816 when the Penal Laws — which were directed against Irish Catholics — were slowly relaxed, Rev. Jeremiah Holland was appointed parish priest of Inchigeela. It is said that he ministered on his own for the greater part of that time to 5,000 people scattered over seventy square miles of hills, crossed by bridle paths. Fr Holland proposed and aided in the construction of two churches and seven schools in the region. The first church he built in Inchigeela was near the site of the present-day national school in the village of Inchigeela. Besides the little oratory on the island of Gougane there are now two large churches in the parish. One of them, that in the village of Ballingeary, was built in 1809 and has been considerably enlarged and improved since. The other church in Inchigeela was built in 1820 and enlarged in 1830. It was re-blessed by parish priest Fr Patrick Hurley in 1889 and named the Church of the Holy Angels and St Finbarr. There is an associated graveyard with nineteenth- and twentieth-century graves. In 1886, Guy's *Directory of County Cork* notes that there were eight schools in the parish, with eighteen teachers. The situation today is very different, with one national school in Ballingeary and one in Inchigeela.

2.7 O'Leary Homeland — Carrignacurra Castle

Just two miles east of Inichigeela on the Lee lies a reminder of revolution in West Cork in the form of Carrignacurra Castle. This is the first castle one meets on the river. Built atop an outcrop, the name Carrignacurra or *Carraig na Corra* means 'the rock of the weir'. It is believed that an eel weir was located immediately below the high rock on which the castle (or to be more correct its tower house) now stands. This was the principal seat of the O'Learys in Uíbh Laoghaire. The other two O'Leary castles in the neighbourhood were Carrignaneela and Drumcarra further east in the Lee Valley. Nature provided an ideal moat with almost impenetrable mountains, rocks and bog in the surrounding landscape.

The arrival of the Anglo-Normans in the year 1169 brought a new generation of castle-type structures to Ireland. During the next sixty years after the initial invasion, the mottes enclosed at the top became one of many signs of Anglo-Norman might in the country. The colonisation of Ireland, especially in the early years, caused a large number of mottes to be constructed in Leinster and east Ulster. The increasing number of Anglo-Norman mottes and the general expansion westwards and southwards into Ireland forced English lordships to consolidate their defensive structures. Hence, a strong tendency to build stone castles developed. Many of the stone castles built in this period can be compared with structures of twelfth-century design in England and Wales.

Southern face of
Carrignacurra Castle; note
the bartizan on the left
(picture: K. McCarthy).

In the early 1300s there was a decline in castle-building, possibly due to the absence of finance available to repair and alter existing castle structures. The Great Famine of 1315-17, warfare and tension accelerated the decline. The plague — the Black Death — also ran rampant between the years 1348 and 1349. Irish society was left devastated. Anglo-Norman authority broke down and their colonies contracted back to the Pale, an area surrounding Dublin. In the early fifteenth century, the English administration offered ten pound subsidies to landowners in the Pale to build small towers to fortify lands. Gaelic areas began to expand, especially in the south. To hold on to their regained land, Gaelic lords also began to build 'tower houses'.

Tower houses like Carrignacurra on the River Lee were a phenomenon in Irish history from the 1400s to the 1600s. The three key ethnic groups in Ireland — Gaelic Irish, English and Gaelicised English — adopted the new style in later centuries. The builders of tower houses kept the vertical emphasis inherited from early Norman stone castles. However, the structures were more rudimentary and more residential than military. The adoption of tower houses by Irish lords represented an anglicisation of Gaelic society and perhaps in part embracing English colonial society.

Carrignacurra Castle is said to have been built *circa* 1570 by Sabina O'Carroll, wife of one of the O'Leary chieftains. The O'Learys were subjects of the McCarthys and were active in many of the Gaelic Irish uprisings during the sixteenth and seventeenth centuries in the Cork

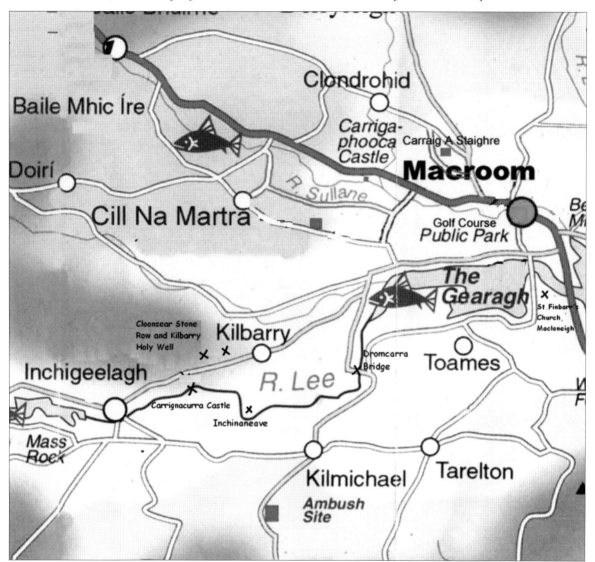

Inchigeela to Macroom, based on *Map of Macroom and the Lee Valley* by Macroom Tourist Office.

area. In 1588 Dermot Oge O'Leary, having previously been pardoned in 1584, was arrested for his part in the Earl of Desmond rebellion against the crown. Hence Dermot's lands were declared forfeited. In 1608 the castle and lands were handed over by James I to the keeping of Francis Goston, an English auditor. However, on this occasion the O'Learys managed to retain possession through a legal loophole. When Teigue O'Leary of Carrignacurra Castle died in 1615, Connogher, his son and heir, claimed hereditary rights. The lands were again forfeited during Oliver Cromwell's protectorate.

   In 1660, the lands were restored under Charles II to the Earl of Clancarty (of the McCarthys of Kilbritain). He issued long leases at low rents to the former O'Leary proprietors. The O'Learys answered the call by the McCarthys to support Catholic King James II in 1689 during his wars in Ireland with the English King and Dutch prince, William of Orange. Indeed, many O'Learys appeared on the army list of James II in Ireland and on the continent. In 1708 the Masters family bought the property from the Hollow Sword Blade Company and

View of the River Lee from the top of Carrignacurra Castle and the makeshift pedestrian bridge across the river (picture: K. McCarthy).

were still in possession of it at the beginning of the nineteenth century. They built a house nearby and invested in the renovation of the tower, renaming it Castle Masters. The castle still survives in a reasonably good state of repair due to partial renovation by Maxim Gormanov in the 1990s and through the efforts of landowner, Derry Kingston.

Carrignacurra Castle is a rectangular four-storey tower, plain in design. The lower courses of quoin stones or corner stones have been robbed. The battlements atop the walls have been completely removed. A corner defensive feature known as a bartizan is supported by three lintels and has a sloping roof. Today, the tower house is on private land and can be accessed through a door in the centre of the east wall at ground–floor level. The door surrounds are now entirely gone. The lobby is covered by a murder hole and gives access to a main ground-floor chamber. The murder hole is a gap in the masonry above the lobby where residents could throw stones or tar down on unwelcome guests. Looking southwards in the lobby is a small guard chamber and just to the north is the base of spiral stairs. The spiral stairs give access to the first, second and third floor levels. The accommodation would have been primitive with no running water. There are garderobes or toilets with wooden seats over stone chutes that are built into the walls.

The upper levels would have been the living and sleeping quarters of the owner. These levels today have an unfinished wooden floor. There are several windows of the narrow lancet type with a few gun loopholes for defence. On the third floor an elaborate fireplace as well as large, decorative windows can be viewed. Overall, Carrignacurra Castle is a noteworthy structure that links the past and the present and highlights the influence of the O'Learys in West Cork through the centuries.

2.8 Breaking the Mould in Inchinaneave

Peg and Tommy O'Leary live in the townland of Inchinaneave or *Inse na Naobh* (Inch of the river rafts). They live two kilometres east of Carrignacurra Castle and five kilometres east along the Lee Valley from Inchigeela, on the border of an extensive forest through which the Lee has carved a path for itself.

Approaching the O'Leary house I passed a Bronze Age standing stone. I stopped to photograph it, thinking about how now it is not located in a rural wilderness but within one hundred metres of a new bungalow. A hundred metres west of the stone lies a Megalithic (Stone Age) tomb known locally as 'the Giant's Grave', but unfortunately I could not locate it due to the fact that the rocky outcrop it is on is overgrown. Tommy O'Leary is proud of the fact that he was brought up in this area and he enthusiastically showed me an Ordnance Survey benchmark on his two-storey house that is built of random rubble masonry. The inscribed arrow points upwards and dates from *circa* 1900.

The landscape of Inchinaneave is striking and rugged. Indeed, the line drawings on the Ordnance Survey Map give no indication of just how extensive and scenic this part of the River Lee Valley is. In this place one gets a better sense of how the landscape was shaped by natural processes and it seems like an unfinished canvas. Places like Gougane Lake and Lough Allua, with their large body of water and the landscaped villages of Ballingeary and Inchigeela, give the observer a 'settling feeling' because of the smoothened landscape. Inchinaneave is quite 'raw', with all its sharp rock outcrops and overgrown vegetation. The valley is still being weathered away and the river and the elements are continually creating new shapes.

In Inchinaneave there is clear evidence of natural processes operating over millions of years. Exposed sandstone deposits reflect a tectonic history. Over 340 million years ago the part of the earth's crust that is now Ireland lay close to the equator. Over millions of years, there was extensive change from land to ocean conditions. With this shift to cooler and wetter climes, thick sequences of sandstone and finer-grained silt-mudstones (old red sandstone) were deposited as sediments in riverine environments and on marginal to upland and mountain areas. Over millions of years, tectonic movement has caused intense folding and faulting of these rocks. As a result, a prominent ridge and trough-fold topography was created in the south west of Ireland.

The River Lee eroded the rock and met with the harder underlying sandstones, so the rivers changed direction to follow west to east folds, as in the case of the River Lee. It is estimated that 250 metres of sandstone have been eroded by rivers in the Cork region over millions of years. Subsequent glaciations also had a strong effect on the land. They determined the surface topography and soil, which societies had to adapt to through the ages. Today much of the soil in the western part of the Lee Valley is peat and peaty gleys. The associated land is best suited for grazing and forests.

At the end of the last ice age, 20,000 years ago, sea level was one hundred metres lower than at present. The ice began to melt and flowed eastwards from the Kerry mountains and from north and north-west regions. Glaciers that were 250 metres thick and the melt water they produced eroded the floor of the Lee Valley. It was the ice itself that carved out the lake beds of Gougane Barra Lake and Lough Allua. During the ice advances enormous amounts of bedrock and soil were moved and redistributed.

The Lee Valley is U-shaped because moving glaciers exposed bedrock and many hills were smoothed by abrasion. In addition, as the ice melted and slowed down, a thick sequence of ice-crushed rock debris (boulder clay or till) and multiple layers of sand, silt, gravel and stones were deposited in the valleys and on the hillsides around Cork City. In recent decades, this has allowed for the exploitation of sand and gravel pits for construction purposes. In Inchinaneave, large pits excavated for their sand reveal boulder clay that is several thousand years old. In addition, the presence of stone-lined drains indicates successful attempts in centuries gone by to drain off the land for agricultural purposes.

O'Leary's farm, Inchinaneave, set against the extensive Lee Valley (picture: K. McCarthy).

Standing stone, Inchinaneave (picture: K. McCarthy).

As well as this, the Lee faces the problems of the local geology at Inchinaneave, as the river is forced to travel south for a kilometre. Extensive sandstone deposits loom on both sides of the river's banks and the river has carved its way through this soft sandstone gauntlet. As soon as the river is able to turn east again it does. Peg O'Leary informs me that the name of the turn is John's Turn, named after John Barry Murphy, a former landowner in the area.

2.9 *Echoes of the Past at Kilbarry*

I was drawn to Kilbarry because of its name, *Cill Barra*, or 'the church of Barry', named after St Finbarre. Here was a connection, another link in the fabled walk of Cork's patron saint from Gougane to Cork harbour. Kilbarry is on the main road from Macroom to Inchigeelagh, another small settlement but with an intriguing past

During an exploration of Kilbarry Hill with the help of local residents Kathleen Lucey, Peggy O'Dea and Ted Cook, stories were shared. The old and ruined Kilbarry church is situated on a terrace near the summit of Kilbarry hill in the townland of Carrignaneelagh. On the map it is noted as a 'burial ground'. The site overlooks two river valleys — that of the River Lee and that of the River Toon (which joins the Lee at the Gearagh) — and lies for the most part in the adjacent parish of Kilnamartyr. It is said Kilbarry church was a Chapel of Ease for Inchigeela, built by the O'Learys and it was probably built at the same time as the O'Leary castles in the area (in the fifteenth to seventeenth centuries AD). In 1700 the Protestant Bishop of Cork, Dive Downes, described the ruins as 'walls of a church or chapel, called Killbarry, the walls built with stone or clay are standing uncovered'. The present day ruins are rectangular and grass and sod-covered throughout. The lower parts of the western wall with its rubble masonry can be seen clearly. The southern wall has been incorporated into the roadside fence. There is no visible trace of the churchyard or burial ground, but through the years local parish priests have continued to bless the site on occasion.

For the most part the archaeology of rural Ireland is protected by nature, and its stories are protected by its people. There is quite a difference between researching rural histories in County Cork and urban histories in Cork City. Histories in the countryside seem to be remembered better. However, in order to discover any place one has to get out there and explore it and chat to the locals. Maps and facts and figures are great to have beforehand, but the reality of the landscape is very different. Trying to find archaeological monuments that appear neatly on a map is, more often than not, very time-consuming. It involves getting lost, retracing your steps a few times, cursing the map and then discovering that the area you have been looking for is overgrown! Kilbarry on a map is quite different from the reality.

Dan Hallisey is a local farmer in the Kilbarry area in the townland of Cloonshear Beg or *Cluain Siar*, which means 'plain of slope of the western aspect'. He gave me a tour of his lands and pointed out that his farmhouse dates to *circa* 1880. Dan is a man used to his local environment and he walks quickly across the rugged ground ahead of me. Multiple sandstone ridges exposed by the elements and especially by glaciation can be seen on his land and the eroding marks are all in a west-east orientation, heading towards the sea. Dan kindly showed me the ancient monuments on his land. First off he revealed a standing stone and then further east a stone row, both of which are marked on the map, but without local knowledge such as Dan's, one would have trouble tracking them down. The standing stone and the stone row, both *circa* 7,000 years old, overlook the Toon River Valley but do run along the crest between the Toon Valley and the valley of the Lee.

The Cloonshear stone row comprised six stones set upright in the ground in a west-east orientation, with the sixth stone taller than the rest. The setting up of these stones required time, strength and careful reasoning. However, the creators of the stone row have left no clues

Kilbarry hill from Kilmichael parish (picture: K. McCarthy).

as to their origin. Dan told me of a legend attached to the area: a long time ago in Celtic Ireland a chieftain was building a castle on the Shehy More — *Seagha Mór* — and the local giants decided to carry large boulders to help the chieftain out. However, the builder died and on hearing the news the giants dropped the boulders while still en route! This is one mythical answer for all the standing stone monuments in Uíbh Laoghaire.

Landscape has different meanings for different people and inspires and appeals to people's imagination in a variety of ways. A good example of this in our study of the Lee Valley is St Finbarre's Holy Well, or Sunday's Well, which is located near Kilbarry. Assisted by Eileen McSweeney, the local landowner, in thrashing down the summer overgrowth, I found it — a spring covered with a slab of stones which appeared to house the holy well. This site is another integral part of the legacy of St Finbarre. There are around 3,000 holy wells in Ireland and they are found in the most interesting of places. There are few parishes in which there is not at least one, but in many parishes there are more. Some of them are shown on the large-scale Ordnance Survey maps but many are not shown.

Many wells like that in Kilbarry are associated with saints like St Finbarre. There are many stories across Ireland that argue that a particular saint used the water of a particular well to baptise his converts and left a blessing on the well. In other cases, saints caused the well to

Cloonshear stone row, July 2006, with local residents Kathleen Lucey, Peggy O'Dea and Dan Hallisey (picture: K. McCarthy).

appear by working a miracle. In some cases, the saint allegedly displaced pagan druids in the area who had previously been in charge of the well. Whether or not these stories have any truth, the water attached to holy wells seems to create an aura or a type of power that has long interested and inspired humankind. Many wells are said to have the power to heal diseases. Cults still flourish and some practices are pre-Christian. Kilbarry's holy well is said to cure toothaches. The locals showing me the sites and sounds of the area, Peggy O'Dea, Kathleen Lucey, Dan Hallisey and Eileen O'Keeffe describe how they were educated to respect the well and not to disturb the waters unnecessarily.

   People usually visit holy wells on a special or prescribed day, especially on the saint's feast day. In Kilbarry's case, Good Friday is the special day. Sunday was also a popular day and *Tobar Domhnaigh*, or 'Sunday's well', is a familiar name for many holy wells, including the Kilbarry well. Scholars researching holy wells have noted that at the beginning of a visit, preliminary prayers were said by the pilgrim, usually five decades of the Rosary. The pilgrim would approach the well and kneeling there say a few more prayers. Then the water would be drunk or a hand would be dipped into it and pilgrims would bless themselves with the water. Often there is a special tree or a bush near the well on which one can hang or put votive offerings such as pictures, statues, or crutches, which can

Kilbarry Holy Well, July 2006, with Peggy O'Dea in the foreground and
Eileen McSweeney and Kathleen Lucey (picture: K. McCarthy).

also be left on the ground near the well. The most common trees are whitethorn, hazel and ash, and formerly oak, but holly, rowan and yew are also found near wells. Leaving an offering is an integral part of a pilgrimage to a holy well. Nowadays, the tendency is to shorten and simplify the ritual.

Close to St Finbarre's well is Peggy O'Dea's Kilbarry post office, which dates to *circa* 1889, while the adjacent National School dates to 1884. The presence of a prefab in the school grounds indicates overcrowding on the one hand, but on the other it means that the village has a consistent and growing youthful population — which I became aware of when Peggy's grandchildren came out to investigate my presence!

The school and post office remind us of Ireland in the late 1870s and 1880s. Charles Stewart Parnell was dominant in Irish in politics and he campaigned for Home Rule in Ireland and established the Irish National Land League. In Cork, relations between landlords and tenants were quite calm in the decade leading up 1877. At the beginning of 1877 prices were excellent for livestock and butter and harvests were good. Home Rule and national independence were far from the minds of the majority of Cork farmers.

In 1877 an agricultural crisis arose that changed the fortunes of the Cork farming community. It was due to a combination of bad weather, poor harvests and falling prices. This was the first of three consecutive sessions of unusual weather that affected Irish farmers. While agricultural output was seriously reduced in Cork, in Connaught and Donegal, overdependence on the potato crop and a primitive economic structure created acute and widespread destitution elsewhere. As the months progressed support for Parnell increased, with thousands of people attending regional meetings across the county. Agrarian protests by tenant farmers continued across the country in the winter of 1880, and in early 1881 Gladstone's liberal government began to tackle the problem.

In the early 1880s the British parliament gave £50,000 to County Cork and £600,000 to Ireland as a whole. The government relied heavily on private relief organisations and on local officials to supply food, and under Disraeli realised that employment was also urgently needed for the labourers and cottiers who were being put under pressure by high rents. In January 1880 the British treasury authorised an advance of £500,000 to Irish landowners and sanitary authorities, for projects normally carried out under the Land Improvement Acts and public health legislation. Kilbarry National School and the post office were built as a consequence of this.

2.10 *The Forgotten Country*

Between Inchinaneave and the Gearagh, the River Lee Valley is extensive. The river now travels in a north-easterly direction for three miles on its own with no third-class road to accompany it. The valley floor is approximately a mile in width and this is an impressive place that clearly shows that it is nature and not man that has shaped the environment here. The results of glaciation are ever present.

Carrignaneelagh or *Carraig na nGeimhleach* — 'the stone house of the house herds' — was the second site of three O'Leary clan castles built in Uíbh Laoghaire in the 1500s, to protect Irish lands from English colonialists. The O'Learys are very much part of the history of this land. Kathleen Lucey brought me to a *lios*, or ringfort, on Kilbarry hill that is not marked on the map. This may have been where the O'Learys lived before they built the castle. Early records for the later castle tower house state that Arthur O'Leary was pardoned in 1573 for whatever part he may have played in the Earl of Desmond rebellion against the English crown, and he received several other pardons up to the year 1587.

In the 1640 Civil Survey, there were thirty-nine landowners in Uibh Laoghaire. There were thirty-six landowners with the surname O'Leary. The largest landholder was Daniel McArthur O'Leary, who held 4,000 acres from Gortsmorane to Carricknamuck, including Kilbarry and Carrignaneelagh. The second-largest landholder was Auliff McDonagh who possessed over 1,000 acres at Carrignacurra and surrounds. He lost all to the crown when he fought in the civil war against the English crown in 1641. All the O'Leary lands were forfeited due to the unrest.

In 1660 under the Acts of Settlement, in association with the restoration of King Charles II, the Carrignaneelagh property was given to the Earl of Clancarty who was made head landlord. Subsequent residents pulled down the castle *circa* 1822. Nothing remains of the castle today. It is said that James Barry was landlord of the area and was High Sheriff of Cork County in the late 1700s. His family may have been directly involved in the taking down of the castle and in the building of a modern dwelling nearby. The fields belonging to the family who currently live there, the Luceys of Kilbarry House, are said to mark its location, and the stones for an extensive and long 'halled' house are said to have come from the castle.

A drawing from 1913 by Michael Holland, a Cork antiquarian, shows the third O'Leary castle, Dromcarra castle or *Drom Carraige* — 'the ridge of the rock' — in a good state of repair. Built on a slight incline but lower down in the Lee Valley than Carrignaneelagh. Dromcarra castle was drawn as a small tower house of three storeys, with remains of battlements, one high

Above: 1 The River Lee in its early stages
in Coom Rua Mountain, part of the Shehy
Mountain range, Co. Cork, July 2006 (picture:
K. McCarthy).

Right: 2 The 'baby' River Lee Valley, Coomroe,
Shehy Mountains, July 2006 (picture: K.
McCarthy).

Above: 3 Natural beauty, Gougane Barra Forest Park, July 2006 (picture: K. McCarthy).

Left: 4 A managed space — Gougane Barra Forest Park, July 2006 (picture: K. McCarthy).

Opposite above: 5 Dereenglass stream, Gougane Barra Forest Park, July 2006 (picture: K. McCarthy).

Opposite below: 6 Sacred spaces — Gougane Barra Forest Park, 2006 (picture: Tony O'Connell).

7 Gougane Barra Lake, field trip with fourth and fifth class of Rockboro National School, Cork, May 2006 (picture: K. McCarthy).

8 The overbearing Shehy Mountains at the entrance to Gougane Barra Forest Park (picture: K. McCarthy).

9 A place of rest, Gougane Barra Graveyard, July 2006 (picture: K. McCarthy).

10 Nineteenth-century stone altar on Gougane Barra pilgrimage island (picture: K. McCarthy).

Above: 13 *Gougane Barra with the Hermitage of St FinBarr*, painting by George Petrie, 1831 (courtesy of: Crawford Municipal Art Gallery).

Right: 14 Artist's interpretation of present-day Ballingeary, interpretative panel at Casadh na Spríde (picture: K. McCarthy).

Opposite above: 11 Ancient spaces — standing stone at Gortafludig, Shehy Mountain range, July 2006 (picture: K. McCarthy).

Opposite below: 12 Stone-walled field systems with residents at Toreenlahard, Shehy Mountain range, July 2006 (picture: K. McCarthy).

15 The road less travelled — access trackway to Dromanallig Clapper bridge, Ballingeary (picture: K. McCarthy).

16 Stained glass window of St Ronan in SS Finbarre's and Ronan's Church, Ballingeary (picture: K. McCarthy).

17 Statue of St Finbarre by Seamus O'Murchada in the churchyard of SS Finbarre's and Ronan's Church, Ballingeary (picture: K. McCarthy).

18 Stained glass window of St Finbarre in SS Finbarre's and Ronan's Church, Ballingeary (picture: K. McCarthy).

19 Casadh na Spríde, Amenity Park, April 2006 (picture: K. McCarthy).

20 Casadh na Spríde during the Féile na Prataí Nua, Ballingeary Community Picnic, July 2006 (picture: K. McCarthy).

21 Scenic Lough Allua from the southern lakeside road, May 2006 (picture: K. McCarthy).

22 From crannógs to farmhouses — the potted 'lakescape' of Lough Allua, May 2006 (picture: K. McCarthy).

23 Elaborate stained glass window of St Finbarre in Inchigeela's Catholic church, the Church of the Holy Angels and St Finbarre (picture: K. McCarthy).

Left: 24 Stained glass window of St Finbarre at St Finbarre's Church, Tooms (picture: K. McCarthy).

Opposite above: 25 Ruins of Glebe House, in operation *c.*1860 to *c.*1885 but burned down in 1920 by Irregulars of the aspiring Free State Government (picture: K. McCarthy).

Opposite below: 26 Contrasting faces of modernity at Inchigeela, Co. Cork, July 2006 (picture: K. McCarthy).

Left: 27 Inchigeelagh Church of Ireland gravestone, July 2006 (picture: K. McCarthy).

Below: 28 O'Leary tomb, Inchigeelagh Church of Ireland church, July 2006 (picture: K. McCarthy).

Opposite above: 29 Inchinaneave House, built *c.*1900 (picture: K. McCarthy).

Opposite below: 30 River Lee at John's Turn, Inchinaneave near Inchigeela, Co. Cork (picture: K. McCarthy).

31 At Kilbarry post office, July 2006, were Gerard Dromey, Julie O'Dea, Josh Pickering, Tim O'Dea, Emer O'Dea and Peggy O'Dea (picture: K. McCarthy).

32 Peaceful and hypnotic flow of the River Lee at Dromcarra South townland, near the Gearagh, Co. Cork (picture: K. McCarthy).

33 Epic landscapes at the Gearagh, July 2006 (picture: K. McCarthy).

34 Ted Cook, Gearagh expert, and Breda Harrington from Kilmurray look over the Florida-like landscape of the Gearagh (picture: K. McCarthy).

Opposite above: 35 Ruins of Annahala settlement, the Gearagh, July 2006 (picture: K. McCarthy).

Opposite below: 36 Winter in the Gearagh, 2004 (picture: Tony O'Connell).

Right: 37 Niamh Casey, Bernard O'Callaghan, Rachel Casey and Bob the dog at Toomes IRA memorial (picture: K. McCarthy).

Below: 38 Lee Bridge, the Gearagh (picture: K. McCarthy).

39 Sunset over Macroom, from Kilmurray, Co. Cork, July 2006 (picture: K. McCarthy).

40 Sunset haze over Carrigadrohid Reservoir, July 2006 (picture: K. McCarthy).

41 View from the big house, Coolcower House, overlooking the River Lee as it enters Carrigadrohid Reservoir (picture: K. McCarthy).

42 N22 western approach road to Macroom, July 2006 (picture: K. McCarthy).

43 Macroom Castle Arch, July 2006 (picture: K. McCarthy).

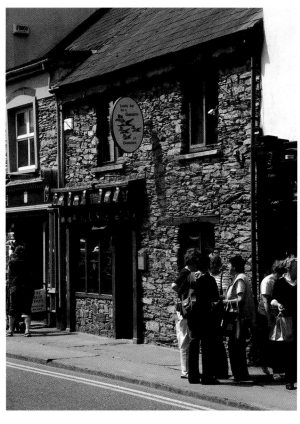

44 Dinneen's pub, Macroom, July 2006 (picture: K. McCarthy).

Above: 45 Ruins of Macroom Castle from Sullane Bridge, July 2006 (picture: K. McCarthy).

Right: 46 Moments in time, Macroom central, *Right:* memorial to Irish patriots at the centre (picture: K. McCarthy).

Left: 47 Ritual progress — from standing stones to speed boats, Carrigadrohid Reservoir, July 2006 (picture: K. McCarthy).

Below: 48 Aghinagh region from Rooves Coachford area, July 2006 (picture: K. McCarthy).

Opposite above: 49 Sunny days, Carrigadrohid river bank, June 2006 (picture: K. McCarthy).

Opposite below: 50 Carrigadrohid Castle during low reservoir levels, July 2006 (picture: K. McCarthy).

Above: 53 Tranquil settings at Inniscarra Reservoir, June 2006 (picture: K. McCarthy).

Right: 54 Memorial to Hugh Maguire, Chief of Fermanagh, killed by English forces on 11 March 1600 at Inniscarra, Co Cork (picture: K. McCarthy).

Opposite above: 51 Coachford suburbia, 2006 (picture: K. McCarthy).

Opposite below: 52 Inniscarra graveyard, 2006 (picture: K. McCarthy).

55 Fourth and fifth class, Rockboro National School, Cork City on a tour of the control room of Inniscarra dam as part of the ESB's educational programme, May 2005 (picture: K. McCarthy).

56 Inniscarra bridge, September 2005 (picture: K. McCarthy).

57 Derry Hurley, landowner and 'caretaker' at Our Lady's Well Walshestown, near Farren, Co. Cork (picture: K. McCarthy).

58 Rooves stone row with landowner and 'caretaker', Finbarr Crowley (picture: K. McCarthy).

59 Tree stumps of the past, Rooves Bridge area, low water, 1990s (picture: Finbarr Crowley).

60 Ballincollig Gunpowder Mills Weir, June 2006 (picture: K. McCarthy).

61 Jenny Webb, local historian, escorting the Green Map Cork group in Ballincollig Gunpowder Mills, January 2006 (picture: K. McCarthy).

62 Carrigrohane Castle, *c*.1850 (picture: Mary O'Brien).

63 Where the River Lee meets the tidal water at Carrigrohane Straight Road, from the top of Cork County Hall, June 2006 (picture: K. McCarthy).

64 Sunlight narratives, Lee fields, July 2006 (picture: K. McCarthy).

chimney and part of a machicolation at one corner. Dromcarra castle was built by the O'Leary family. In 1627 the lands of Dromcarra castle belonged to Auliffe, son of Conor O'Leary, who died in 1600. Teige O'Leary was his son and heir. In the Muskerry Survey of 1654-55, the castle was described as being badly damaged. The structure was deemed dangerous by its owner, who tore it down in 1968. A pile of grey stones now remains, with nature attempting to take the land back.

The southern side of the Lee Valley is particularly impressive as it gradually slopes down to the river. At one point there is a break in the southern side of the valley as the Cooldoraragha River joins the Lee and becomes a tributary. It is this river that passes through the famous parish and village of Kilmichael. The local church, a nineteenth-century building just east of the village, offers great views of the Lee and overlooks the townlands of Inchineil, Dromcarra South and Dromcarra North. Inchineill or *Inse Uí Neil* means 'river Inch of O'Neill'. Dromcarra, or *Drom Carra*, means 'ridge of the causeway or stepping-stones'. At the eastern side of Dromcarra South, the Lee turns north, unable to carve a path through Cooldaniel hill. In Cooldaniel stands another holy well, recently revamped and enclosed by an elaborate well house.

The Lee and Dromcarra Bridge form the boundary of Uíbh Laoghaire parish and the parish of Kilmichael (Church of St Michael). Further north on the western side of the valley, the townlands of Gortmoorane, Milleen and Teerquay are encountered before the Lee enters the Gearagh. On the eastern side of the valley stretching north-east from Kilmichael are the townlands of Cooldorragha, Moneycusker, Cooldaniel and Inchisine, Cooldorragha, or *Cúl Dorcha* — 'dark hill-back with northerly slope — and Moneycusker, or *Muine a'Choscair* — 'thicket of strife or slaughter'. Here are the ruins of an old parish church and graveyard, built in a ringfort called Lisheenacluvane or *Lisín a'Chlumhain* — 'little fort of the hairy man'.

Kilbarry House, July 2006, with local farmer, Tim Buckley and Ted Cook, environmental expert, Kilbarry (picture: K. McCarthy).

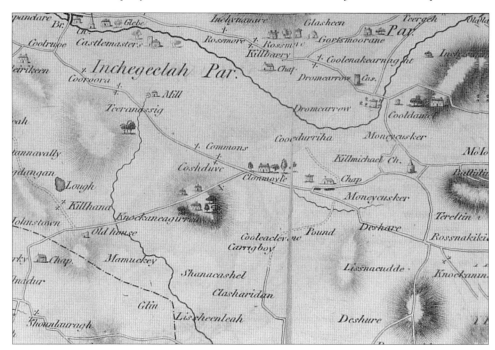

Section of Grand Jury Map of County Cork in 1811 showing Kilbarry and surrounding areas (source: Cork City Library).

Cooldaniel or *Cú Domhaill* means 'Daniel's recess or hill-back'. On the townland's western side is St Michael's Well. Inchisine, or *Inse Saighme*, means 'River Inch of the attack or charge'. The townland is located in the parish of Macloneigh or *Magh Cluain Eich*, meaning 'plain of the dell (hollow) of the steed'.

In 1837 Samuel Lewis noted that Kilmichael parish was partly in the western divisions of the barony of East Carbery but chiefly in the barony of West Muskerry, six miles (SSW) from Macroom. In 1837 the parish had 6,166 inhabitants and comprised 20,835 statute acres, as allocated under the Church of Ireland Tithe Act. About half the land of the parish was deemed good for pasture, one third was deemed arable, and the remainder was classified as bog and mountain. The geology was described as slatey and containing indications of copper, particularly in the bed of the river. Lewis noted the presence of a local constabulary police station.

In 1837 the principal gentry houses were Cooldaniel, that of J. Barter, and Carrigbuoy, belonging to E. Barrett and B. Sweete in whose demesne there were lakes with great numbers of swans and waterfowl. In 1837, Lewis noted that on Sweete's lands an ancient rath or ringfort had been investigated, in which a bag of copper coins and several apartments, communicating by narrow passages, were discovered. There was a Protestant rectory as well as a vicarage in the area, but these were made a part of the rectory and vicarage of Macloneigh in 1797. The local Protestant church was described as a small ancient building, while there is no record of a glebe house for the Protestant clergy. In terms of Roman Catholic divisions in 1837, Kilmichael was the head of a union or district, comprising also Macloneigh, Kilmurry, and Dunisky, and containing three chapels, two in Kilmichael and one in Macloneigh. About twenty children were educated in the parochial school, aided by a donation of £12 per annum from the rector. In addition, there were four private schools in the area, in which about 140 children were educated.

Ted Cook, local resident and the ruins of Dromcarra Castle, July 2006 (picture: K. McCarthy).

River Lee flowing under Dromcarra bridge, July 2006, boundary of Uíbh Laoghaire and Kilmichael parish (picture: K. McCarthy).

Dromcarra South, Co. Cork (picture: K. McCarthy).

2.11 Remembering Kilmichael

'They shall be spoken of among their people, the generations shall remember them and call them blessed.' [14]

Kilmichael is a quaint settlement, a crossroads where J. Collins Foodstore, Furlong Flour, a grotto, a school and a three-bed cottage sporting a 'for sale' sign all combine as signs of urbanisation. The surrounding area is scattered with more one-off two-storey housing bungalows as well as twentieth-century farmsteads. Travelling two miles south of Kilmichael on the road to Shanlaragh village and Kealkill, one climbs the crest of the southern side of the valley of the Lee. It is here that the Rev. C. O'Brien, parish priest of Kilmichael, unveiled an elaborate monument on 10 July 1966, dedicated to the memory of the Kilmichael Ambush in 1920.

Judging from the size of the memorial, it is clear that it is meant to constantly remind inhabitants of Kilmichael parish of their history. The existing interpretive panels also link the event and describe its important contribution to Irish history. Unlike the history of places already discussed, such as Gougane Barra, Lough Allua and Carrigacurra Castle, the Kilmichael ambush memorial relates to a recent past, to events from eighty years ago. At that time, several Corkmen used the environment to help them focus their concerns about the situation that

Ireland found itself in. The Kilmichael ambush site was one of several points of attack in southern Ireland in a quest for Irish independence from the British Empire during the Irish War of Independence of the early twentieth century.

On 28 November 1920 the Black and Tans left the town of Macroom and were unexpectedly met by the Flying Column led by Republican general Tom Barry at Kilmichael. Tom Barry had enlisted in the British Army during the First World War and served in Mesopotamia. He returned to Ireland in 1919 and became a prominent member of the Irish Republican Army during the War of Independence. The ambush area he chose was and still is in the centre of a bleak and barren countryside, a bogland mixed together with heather and rocks. It was poor terrain for an ambushing unit because of the lack of roadside ditches. A number of scattered rocky eminences of varying sizes provided the appropriate cover.

The Auxiliaries, named the Black and Tans because of the colour of their uniforms, were stationed at Macroom castle. Although they were stationed in Macroom, outside of the West Cork IRA Brigade area, they regularly raided the area, taking in Coppeen, Castletownkenneigh and Dunmanway. A week before the ambush, thirty-six men came together at Clogher to be trained in guerrilla warfare tactics by General Barry. At 2a.m. on Sunday 28 November 1920 the same thirty-six came together at O'Sullivan's of Ahilnane, northwest of Ballineen. Here, Fr O'Connell of Ballineen heard the men's confessions and gave them his blessing. Each man was armed with one rifle and thirty-five rounds of ammunition, and the column had a few revolvers as well as two mills bombs, which had been captured at a previous ambush.

At 3a.m. the men were told that they were going to attack the Auxiliaries on the road between Dunmanway and Macroom. Just before their arrival at Kilmichael, sixteen-year-old Pat Deasy of the Bandon Battalion joined the column. He had been ill with the flu two days earlier and had been forbidden to join. The column began their march avoiding the roads and houses and they reached the site at Kilmichael just before dawn.

Two unarmed scouts were waiting north of the site where the ambush would take place and at the Dunmanway end there was another scout. The men stayed in their positions throughout the day, from 9a.m. to 4p.m., when the Auxiliaries' approach was communicated to the Flying Column. In fact, it was a horse and side-car carrying five armed volunteers that entered the area, followed by the Auxiliaries. The five volunteers were Irish men on their way to join the Flying Column for a week's training. There had been a mix-up of dates and the five were a week late. However, there was a narrow lane nearby and Barry instructed the volunteers to go up the lane, which they did, staying there for the duration of the ambush.

As the first lorry of Black and Tans came around the turn, Barry — dressed in a volunteer tunic — stood facing it on the road. Because of the fading light, the British mistook him for a British officer and slowed down. As they did, Barry blew on his whistle and tossed the mill bomb, which landed in the lorry killing the driver. The No. 1 Section dealt with those remaining in the lorry, with the Auxiliaries firing shots and the Flying Column pouring lead into them. Soon, some of the Auxiliaries were on the road and the fight became a hand-to-hand one. The Auxiliaries in the second lorry were taken on by the No. 2 Section and soon, those in the first lorry had been defeated. Seeing this, Barry and his three companions moved from their post, along the grass verge, to ambush the second lorry from behind, unknown to the Black and Tans.

The Auxiliaries then shouted 'We surrender' twice and some threw away their rifles. The No. 2 Section that was fighting this group accepted the plea and three inexperienced members of the section stood up. The Auxiliaries were ready and fired, killing Michael McCarthy and Jim O'Sullivan and seriously wounding a young Pat Deasy, who died later. Tom Barry gave an order to open fire, killing the remaining Auxiliaries.

---

14. Inscription on Kilmichael Ambush Memorial.

Four men were then sent for a door to take away the injured youth, six were ordered to man protection positions and eighteen were to disarm the Auxiliaries and take papers from them, while the remainder prepared to burn the lorries. An unarmed scout was sent for a priest and doctor. The other two collected any personal items belonging to O'Sullivan and McCarthy and made preparations for the removal of their bodies. Pat Deasy was borne away and the column commenced drilling to stop shock from setting in. They were now ready to begin the long march to Granure.

However, back at the ambush site, the Kelly and O'Donoghue families who lived nearby were subject to the Auxiliaries' retaliation when they travelled from Macroom on the day following the ambush. Jim Coughlan, the local postmaster, was taken away because as a government official he was obliged to report on the ambush, which he had failed to do. He was imprisoned in Cork Gaol for three months. On the Tuesday following the ambush, Auxiliaries returned to Kilmichael and went into the bar of the same name, where the only person present was Denny O'Sullivan of Toames. They took him out and shot him. Following these incidents, the men of the area stayed on the run until the interest in the area faded.

In all, seventy-five men were involved in the Kilmichael ambush and they were from all parts of West Cork, including Dunmanway, Clonakilty, Bantry, Bandon, Ballineen, Newcestown and Coppeen. Tom Barry went on to oppose the Anglo-Irish Treaty and supported the Republican side during the Civil War. Barry, like other leading Republicans, was arrested by the Eamonn de Valera administration in 1934. He called for a war against England in 1936 and demanded that the IRA should not take part in the defence of the Spanish Republic. Tom Barry resigned his position on the Army Council in 1937 and ceased to be an IRA activist in 1940. He was unsuccessful as an independent candidate in Cork in 1946. He is the author of *Guerrilla Days in Ireland.* (1949), *The Reality of the Anglo-Irish War 1919-21* (1974) and a pamphlet refuting much of Liam Deasy's *Towards Ireland Free.*

Kilmichael Ambush Memorial, unveiled in 1966 (picture: K. McCarthy).

'Men of the South', a painting by Seán Keating recalling the flying columns of the War of Independence (courtesy, Crawford Municpal Art Gallery Cork).

Command-Post Memorial, near the Kilmichael Ambush Memorial (picture: K. McCarthy).

2.12 *Transforming Landscapes —*
Building the River Lee Hydro-Electric Scheme

Three miles to the south-west of Macroom lies the townland Teerqay or *Tír gCaoth*, which means 'land of quagmires' — not a very appealing name. Here the River Toon meets the Lee, adding to its body of energy. Toon Bridge provides access to the region of Kilbarry hill. However, the townland's name does not do justice to the area, which is better known as The Gearagh or *An Ghaorthadh*, meaning 'wooded glen'.

The Gearagh is a unique natural environment that has river channels flowing through an ancient forest system. The area is a 'miniature Florida swamp', that is about three miles long. There are over one hundred species of flowering plants and ferns and wild fowl to be found. In 1987 the area was declared a statutory nature reserve under the Wildlife Act of 1976 in cooperation with the ESB, who owned the land. The ESB's quest to provide electricity to the general population has had and continues to have an overbearing influence on the landscape in the Lee Valley an on how Corkonians see the valley today.

The Lee Hydro-Electric Scheme of the 1950s changed much of the topography of the River Lee Valley. Electricity is an energy source that many of us take for granted. It is an energy that can change landscapes depending on how it is created and distributed. The pylons, for example, can alter the beauty of a rural scene, but they also enable us to light up public spaces, our homes, our streets, our shop fronts, and are beneficial to us in terms of safety and comfort.

It was in the late 1870s that the electromagnetic effect previously experimented with by Michael Faraday in the 1820s was brought to a new level. Powerful generators that were for practical use were devised to generate electricity. The world's first really successful power station and electricity distribution network was Thomas Edison's Pearl Street plant in New York, which began working on 4 September 1882. In Cork, Brother Dominic Burke, a Christian Brother and a leading educationalist in the city, had a strong interest in electricity. He lived and taught at the North Monastery School. When Pope Pius IX celebrated the silver jubilee of his episcopacy, Burke honoured the occasion by erecting a huge lamp on the grounds of the North Monastery.

During the 1883 Cork Industrial Exhibition, stalls demonstrating electric light machinery, telegraphs, telephones, magic lantern displays and power transmissions attracted huge crowds who wanted to observe these previously unseen scientific displays. One of the highlights of the exhibition was an electrically run tramcar with eight wheels that ran around the stalls and sideshows of the vast hall. When the exhibition ended, the corporation asked city engineer M.J. McMullen to find out about the cost of providing urban lighting and public tramcars. Electricity first illuminated the streets of urban Irish settlements like Cork in the 1890s — in 1898 the corporation of Cork funded and established an electric tramway system for the city.

In the 1920s electricity was still only available to certain parts of the Irish populace. In 1925 there were forty electrical companies in Ireland and there was no cooperation or coordination between the suppliers. Three years previously, in 1922, the birth of the Irish Free State coincided with the demand for the provision of electricity to the wider public. Between 1923 and 1929 an Electricity Supply Bill was proposed in order to establish Ireland's Electricity Supply Board. The state board was founded on 9 March 1927, focusing on the countrywide distribution of electricity and the promotion of its use. It was further proposed that Ireland's principal rivers could be ideal sources of hydro-electric power.

Dr T.A. McLaughlin, a young Irish engineer, and Dr Patrick McGilligan, Minister of Industry and Commerce in the Free State Government, were consulted when it came to harnessing the Shannon to produce electricity in a hydro-electric plant. The complex that is now at Ardnacrusha was developed and President W.T. Cosgrave opened it on 22 July 1929. The Second World War slowed down the expansion of the electricity industry. There were other priorities, like food rationing, and it was difficult enough to maintain an electricity supply for customers,

Tree stumps at The Gearagh from the Lee Hydro-Electric Scheme (picture: K. McCarthy).

Flooded Annahala routeway, The Gearagh, July 2006 (picture: K. McCarthy).

let alone to develop a rural electricity scheme. In the post-war years other resources like turf-peat were used. Ten burning stations were built and they used imported fuels like coal and oil. The initial stages of electrification were confined to large towns and large villages.

Between the years 1943 and1946 the first rural electrification scheme was initiated in County Dublin. On 22 December 1947 the area of Curaheen near Inniscarra with its one hundred houses was the first electrification project to be finished in County Cork. Between the years 1947 and 1959 a further sixty-eight areas in County Cork were connected to an electricity network (O'Donoghue, 1996).

During that period a hydro-electric scheme for the River Lee began to be discussed. Between the years 1943 and 1953 the Lee was surveyed and water-flow measurements were taken at key locations in the valley. The questions that were asked were: what land would have to be flooded if a reservoir was to be constructed? How many houses on the land would have to be submerged? What roads and bridges would have to be replaced?

In 1943 a geological survey of the Lee Valley was completed. Borings and trial pits were sunk in 1944 and in 1948. In 1948 the ESB decided that the Lee could offer an economical return. The construction of two stations was proposed, one at Inniscarra and the other at Carrigadrohid. Preparatory designs were drawn up and in July 1948 an aerial survey of the land needed was completed. The land required for the scheme was inspected and valued by the land purchase section.

The Electricity (Supply) Act (Amendment) of 1945 granted significant legal powers to the ESB to acquire lands for proposed hydro-electric schemes. The River Lee scheme was approved on 1 December 1949. The ESB acquired 4,485 acres of land, which ranged from ordinary agricultural land to rough scrub-covered marsh, to wooded areas. A total of 3,500 acres were to be flooded out. The remaining 985 acres either remained in ESB ownership or were resold by the board.

The total cost of the land acquisition came to £ 415, 083. A total of thirty-nine houses, one shop and one hotel — the Angler's Rest at Roove's Bridge near Coachford — had to be destroyed. There were mixed reactions among the owners whose lands and property were acquired. The board's valuer visited each landowner and compensation was offered.

After much negotiation, landowners were compensated according to how much and what kind of land they were losing. There was no organised opposition to the Hydro-Electric Scheme. The communities affected were spread across seven parishes and two different dioceses. Planning objections were unheard of and many people did not have enough money to fight the scheme. The Lee Valley Hydro-Electric Scheme began in February 1953. All scrub and trees growing below high water level were cut so no tree would project upwards. The timber was sold to timber merchants and building materials from destroyed dwellings were salvaged. All of the buildings were demolished in controlled explosions.

In May 1953 work at Carrigadrohid Dam began and in October 1956 the associated reservoir was filled in. Six hundred men were employed to do manual labour on the scheme, and they were especially needed to prepare the rock face. Wooden buildings to accommodate 123 workers, and a temporary canteen and recreation facilities for 250 workmen and staff were built. A series of temporary wooden bungalows were also developed for married staff. On Tuesday 23 October 1956 the sluice gates at Carrigadrohid were lowered and flooding of the valley began. The river rose five feet per day in the specially created reservoir. On 26 October 1956 the sluice gates at Inniscarra Dam and the adjacent reservoir began to be filled.

2.13 *The Gearagh – Landscapes within a Landscape*

One of the areas most significantly influenced by the Lee Hydro-Electric Scheme was The Gearagh, an area that extends eastwards and southwards from Dromcarra Bridge and about seven kilometres towards the Lee Bridge. Charles Smith, an antiquarian, noted in 1750:

This river has its course here, interrupted with islands and a deep boggy tract, until it runs to the bridge of Ballynaclassen. These islands are covered, mostly with oak, ash, hazel and birch; at the feet of which grow fern, polypodium, and water drop worth. Here are great quantities of several kinds of water fowl, in their season, as bitterns, cranes, duck and mallard, teal, &c.. These bogs have been attempted to be drained, but it was found impracticable. In one called Anaghaly, is about three acres of ground, on which is excellent limestone, that supplies the town of Macroom, the western inhabitants of this barony and Carbery, with lime for manure and building. [15]

The Lee Hydro-Electric Scheme destroyed half the original area of the Gearagh. This area is the only extensive alluvial woodland in Ireland or Britain, or indeed Western Europe, west of the Rhine. For this reason it is a unique site and has been designated as a Statutory Nature Reserve. The Gearagh qualifies as a priority habitat under Annex I of the European Habitats Directive. The international importance of the site is recognised by its designation both as a Ramsar site (a United Nations Area of Conservation) and as a biogenetic reserve. The adjacent reservoir is also a wildfowl sanctuary.

The wooded part of The Gearagh is largely undisturbed due to the inaccessible nature of the terrain. Annahala Bridge provides a bridge into this special site. The townland Annahala or *Eanaigh Gheala*, means 'white marshes'. The name comes from the adjacent outcroppings of limestone and the worked quarry, which was filled in during the flooding of the area for the Lee scheme. During my recent visit the primary path via the old bridge, which gives access to the heart of the Gearagh complex, was flooded out. In order to get across, walking barefoot was the order of the day. I was fortunate enough on that occasion to be shown part of the site by Ted Cook, a resident of Kilbarry Hill and tour guide with the Heritage Council — and clearly a passionate fan of this environment. Ted explains that the Gearagh can also be a very dangerous place to those not familiar with it. It is very easy to get lost. There are deep areas and muddy banks, and floods do occur regularly.

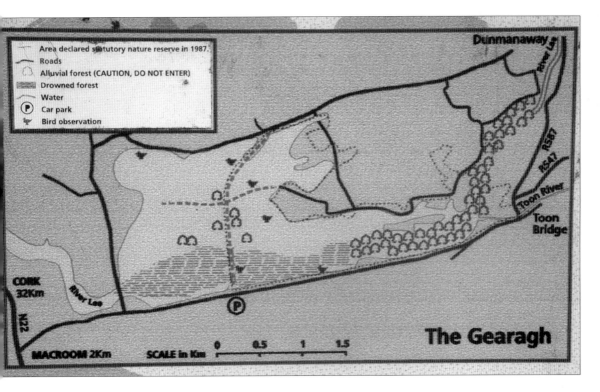

ESB interpretive sign of the Gearagh area.

Enjoying the July 2006 sunshine in The Gearagh were Colm O'Halloran and Anne Dineen from Blarney (picture: K. McCarthy).

The Gearagh occupies a wide flat valley on a bed of limestone overlain with sand and gravel. The adjacent valley walls are of Old Red Sandstone. This unusual area has formed where the Lee breaks into a complex network of channels (two to six metres wide) that meander through a series of wooded islands. The alluvial (riverine) woodland is wet, marshy and overgrown, an environment ideal for creating ecosystems (systems that change every week). One can explore the effects of biodiversity change here, as well as the haven for flora and fauna that has been created. The Gearagh has many landscapes, from macro-level to micro-level.

The area has probably been wooded sine the Post-Glacial era, that is, since the end of the last Ice Age, which ended around 10,000 years ago. Frequent flooding continues to enhance its character. Originally this area of alluvial woodland extended as far as the Lee Bridge. Unfortunately, between 1954 and 1955 extensive tree-felling and flooding were carried out in the eastern part of The Gearagh to facilitate the operation of a hydro-electric scheme. Approximately sixty percent of the former woodland was lost.

The Gearagh's soil structure consists of dry alluvium and supports an almost closed canopy of oak, ash and birch. The 'understorey' is of hazel, holly and hawthorn. Willows and alder are largely limited to channel margins and waterlogged areas. The ground flora reflects the damp nature of the woodland. In spring, ramsons and wood anemone are widespread. Later in the year, other species appear, including bugle, pignut, Irish spurge, tufted hair grass, enchanter's nightshade and meadowsweet. Plant species of particular interest within the woodland are wood club-rush, bird cherry and buckthorn. These species are scarce in Ireland. Lichen communities are well developed in the lower levels (Bryophyte levels) of the woodland. Variations in the flora occur locally, where drainage is hindered and where tree clearance has occurred. In truth, the entire area has a remarkably wild character, with many fallen trees blocking the channels, so that access both on foot and by boat is difficult.

15. Smith, C., *A History of Cork* (Cork), p.190.

Part of the ruins of Annahala Bridge (picture: K. McCarthy).

Within the reservoir, the former extent of the woodland can still be seen at times of low water. The cut stumps of larger trees are still prominent. At least five species of pondweed occur in the reservoir, including two species that are uncommon in Ireland. At low water levels a diverse 'ephemeral' flora develops on the exposed mud. Species here include water purslane, knotgrasses, trifid bur-marigold, marsh yellow-cress and six-stamened waterwort.

In The Gearagh the river channels have also created marginal alluvial grassland in places. Wildfowl graze these grasslands, as well as some semi-improved grasslands within the site. Extensive pastures of mudwort, a rare plant, occur on the mudflats along the reservoir. Otters are frequently found throughout the site. The Gearagh supports part of an important wintering bird population: the area most utilised by birds also extends east of the site, towards Cork City (Carrigadrohid). Whooper swans as well as wigeon, teal, and tufted duck are regularly seen here. Golden plover also utilise the site on occasion, while there is a regular flock of dunlin, a species not usually found at inland sites. A late summering flock of mute swan is also regularly observed. Great crested grebe and tufted duck breed in small numbers here, while there is an undomesticated flock of greylag geese.

Cattle graze in some areas but their impact is very localised. In the past, coppicing was practiced over most of the area. Little felling has occurred since the early 1950s and the installation of the Hydro-Electric Scheme. The least disturbed part of woodland is in the upper reaches of The Gearagh. Tree regeneration is occurring around the reservoir, which may replace some of the lost woodland.

The Gearagh has been a nature reserve for twenty years under the direction of the National Parks and Wildlife Service and the ESB (who own the site). It is a truly spectacular place. It is isolated and undisturbed, with no management or policing of the forest at all. Supporters and regular visitors to the Gearagh are worried about its conservation and wildlife, fishing and hunting. As one regular visitor I encountered in my travels noted, *'To conserve the Gearagh? Local knowledge is important... people in the region need to act to protect what is on their own doorstep. Many local people don't realise the importance of what they have got'.*

2.14 *Further Footprints of a Saint —*
St Finbarre's Church, Macloneigh

In the eastern section of The Gearagh or in the northern section of the basin created for the River Lee by the Hydro-Electric Scheme, the river travels around the tip of a small type of peninsula. The Lee Bridge, built in the 1950s, goes from the R584, the regional road to Uíbh Laoghaire, into the parish of Macloneigh. The townland names adjacent to the Gearagh and Carrigadrohid Reservoir include Toombog, Coolcour, Farranavarrigane and Inchinashingane. Toombog, or *Currach na d'Tuamacha*, means 'bog of the burial mounds'; Coolcour, or *Cúil Cobhair*, means 'recess of froth' from the joining of the rivers Lee and Sullane; Farranavarrigane, or *Fearann Aimheirgin*, means 'Amergin's holding' and Inchinashingane, or *Inse na Seangan*, can be translated as 'River Inch of the ants'.

Travelling over the Lee Bridge towards Tooms, there is a track immediately on the left that leads to the site of another ancient church named after St Finbarre. Here is another link to the saint's walk. The ruins of the old church, of unknown construction date, are situated in the Cill Field, or *Pairc na Cille*, meaning 'field of the church'. The area is also known as *Tuaim Musraighe*, meaning 'burial ground of Muskerry'. The ruins of the church are atop a rocky outcrop overlooking the Lee, and anyone passing through this area centuries ago would have seen the imposing structure.

At nearly twenty-three by seven metres, St Finbarre's church was a substantial and spacious structure and must have sheltered a large crowd. Today, three quarters of the limestone walls are intact and stand three metres high. The western and eastern gables stand at least six metres high. The northern section of the church walls is completely flattened. The extant walls are currently being renovated and conserved by the Historic Monuments Advisory Committee in association with Cork County Council, who have cut away much vegetation, revealing an elaborate ancient building. The conservation project, which is funded by the advisory committee, is part of a wider survey of ancient churches in Ireland. Archaeologist Eamonn Cotter, who is involved in the project, has observed that the architectural style of Macloneigh church dates to the fifteenth to sixteenth century.

The existing walls are a metre thick with a rubble interior, but they are dressed or shaped on the exterior. There is evidence of limestone mortar holding the walls together, but the walls are in danger of collapsing, so conservation is very important. There is only one decorative window, which lies behind the altar. There is almost nothing left of the roof. The extant walls show no signs of corbels or roof supports, even though the wall at the back of the church has a ledge as if it supported timber. There are also putlog holes or scaffolding holes in the exterior face of that wall.

The building is medieval-looking and a papal decree from 1199 refers to a parish in this area. In addition, there are many gravestone 'stumps' with no markings, which is evidence that the site was also an unbaptised children's burial ground, a *cillín*. They may also mark the remains of local victims of the Great Famine. Irish archaeological scholars suggest that *cillíns* may also mark the site of early Christian churches. St Finbarre's church could therefore be an early link to St Finbarre.

The earliest grave to be seen in the associated graveyard dates to 1789 and is that of Denis Kelly. The most recent grave dates to 1985 and is that of Ellen O'Riordan from Kilcullen, Donoughmore. A couple of nineteenth-century burials are also present. One grave plot in the middle of the church, which is surrounded by railings, appears to be nineteenth-century in origin, which suggests that the church was well out of use by that point in time. A gravestone in the shape of the cross of Geofrey O'Connor, who died in 1853, is supported by an iron bar. Another ornate family plot is that of the Buckley family. The grass is very overgrown and if it were cut, more graves would be revealed. I would even suggest that there are layers of burials in this graveyard spanning at least a thousand years. Young trees and a wired fence enclose the overall site.

Ancient ruins of St Finbarre's Church, Macloneigh, Co. Cork (picture: K. McCarthy).

Altar window, late Medieval architecture of St Finbarre's Church, Macloneigh (picture: K. McCarthy).

Overgrown graveyard of St Finbarre's Church, Macloneigh, Co. Cork (picture: K. McCarthy).

St Finbarre's Church, Tooms (picture: K. McCarthy).

   In terms of a Roman Catholic church in the area, today the nearest one is at Tooms, which is in the parish of Kilmichael. It was built in 1831 and in the last year has undergone conservation works producing a fine modern church. The edifice is dedicated to St Finbarre and at the back of the church there is a stained glass window to the saint. The window is also dedicated to the memory of a local family, the McSweeneys.

   From the townlands of Toomsbog and Tooms East, there are extensive views of the Gearagh all the way west to Shehy More and to the east into Aghinagh Parish, which lies to the south east of Macroom town. There are seven ringforts (marked on the Ordnance Survey maps), located to the south and south-west of St Finbarre's church in Tooms on the very scenic southern side of the Lee Valley and they are evidence that there was a population in the area at least one thousand years ago is. Apart from the ringforts, Bronze Age standing stones are common in this area. There is also a number of quaint old farmhouses and outhouses, all of which lie adjacent to modern houses and the Macroom 'Numico' complex, a factory that specialises in the production and research of 'baby food and clinical nutrition'. Its buildings stand out from the landscape when viewing it from higher ground in Tooms.

III

THE FUNCTIONAL RIVER

3.1 Macroom — the Frontier Town

This place [Macroom] is situated on the frontier of a very wild country, being all rocky and barren to the west, and mountainous to the north. [16]

Macroom is situated on an open vale surrounded by moderately high hills and enlivened by the meandering course of the River Sullane, which can be crossed by an arched bridge adjoining the castle. About a mile below the bridge the tributary of the River Lany enters the Sullane. There is another stone bridge of nine arches here. Con O'Leary's scrap yard marks the point where the River Sullane meets Carrigadrohid Reservoir or the River Lee.

Macroom is said to have gotten its name from the Irish for 'a crooked oak', because of a large oak tree that formerly grew in the market square. The settlement originated with the erection of a castle, which was built in the reign of John by the Anglo-Norman family of the De Cogan (*circa* 1200). This castle subsequently became the property of the McCarthys and was repaired and improved by Teigue McCarthy, who died there in 1565. During the time of the plantation of Munster in the late 1500s the McCarthys were the King's local 'stewards' and were also known as Lords of Muskerry. They were obliged to encourage the settlement of several Protestant English families in the Macroom area. The new families who took up residence were the Hardings, Fields, Terrys, Goulds and Kents. The colonisation led very quickly to large-scale Anglicisation, which was an attempt to destabilise Irish society by introducing new English laws and traditions

In the first two decades of the 1600s the Munster plantation was successful in its endeavours to bring more planters to Ireland. By 1611 5,000 planters were recorded in Munster, and this rose to 22,000 by 1641. With this colonisation came an influx of skilled workers, which led to an increase in the country's productivity. However, in the opening decades of the seventeenth century, the English government began to have problems with the people they had planted there. It seems that many of the English planters were intermarrying with Irish women and no longer felt completely loyal to the crown. In 1601 Munster's English administration became apprehensive that the owner of Macroom castle, Dermot McCarty, attempted a revolt. Sir Charles Wilmot took the structure during a long siege in 1602. On that occasion the Irish garrison were compelled by an accidental fire to abandon the fortress.

---

16. Smith, C., *A History of Cork* (Cork), p.181.

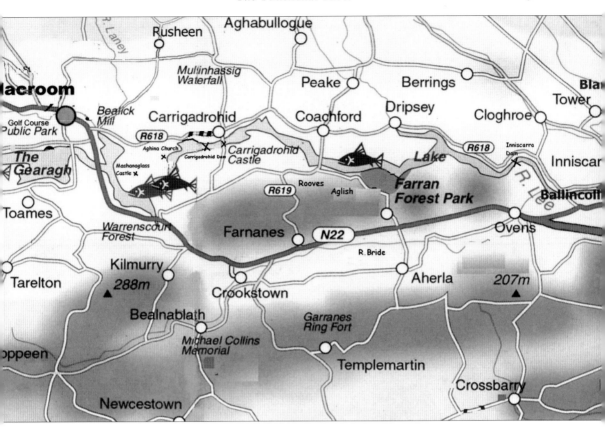

Macroom to Ballincollig, based on *Map of Macroom and the Lee Valley* by Macroom Tourist Office.

In 1624 Charles I, the new king, was more interested in promoting himself and his position than in pursuing the needs of local people. This could be observed in Cork in the late 1620s and early 1630s when campaigns by Protestant leaders in Munster — asking for prominent roles in political and economic life in England — were ignored, and false promises were made. Over time this had a negative effect on the financial and social position of many Protestant settlers in Cork.

From 1633 to 1640 Charles I appointed Thomas Wentworth to promote the throne in Britain and Ireland. He began curtailing the privileges of both Catholic and Protestant leaders which led to further dissatisfaction among Protestant groups. In April 1642 a decision was taken under the leadership of Lord Muskerry that the McCarthys would blockade Cork City. In August 1642 it was decided to besiege a prominent English castle of Liscarroll in North Cork. This castle was won back after thirteen days by pro-crown supporters.

In 1650 the Catholic Bishop of Ross, Beotius MacEgan, assembled an Irish army of 4000 men and 300 horses from the western part of the county to relieve Clonmel, which was at that time besieged by Oliver Cromwell. The approach of Lord Broghill with 2,000 of the parliamentarian cavalcade caused the bishop to set fire to the castle. The bishop lost his campaign to Lord Broghill. Ireton, who was soon afterwards made President of Munster, despatched a party from Kilkenny that burned both the castle and the town.

In 1654 Oliver Cromwell gave Sir William Penn, a distinguished English admiral, a considerable estate — the castle and manor of Macroom in County Cork. Penn's son was also William, and he was born in 1644 in Tower Hill, London. William Junior was educated at Oxford. However, he was expelled for non-conformity, reputedly because of his contact with the Quaker movement.

He then went to France to study for two years at the Protestant University of Saumur before returning to London to study law at Lincoln's Inn. On the accession of King Charles II in the 1660s William Penn Senior was dispossessed and compensated with lands in Shanagarry, County Cork. In 1667 his father, the admiral, sent William Junior to manage the estate. While in East Cork he converted to Quakerism and it is known that in 1667 he visited the walled town of Cork in 1667 and attended a Quaker meeting there. William Penn went on to become the author of a large number of literary works and eventually emigrated to America, where he was instrumental in establishing the state of Pennsylvania, which was named after him.

In May 1703 the Hollow Sword Blade Company purchased the castle and lands and the rights to it were passed from one to the other down the years. While doing field work in Macroom for his *Topographical Dictionary of Ireland* Samuel Lewis observed that until the 1830s Macroom castle was the joint property of the Earl of Bandon and Robert Hedges Eyre, and that comparatively little work was done on it during this time. Under Eyre, considerable progress was made in the improvement of the castle. He converted it into an elegant modern mansion that the old towers were incorporated into. It was a spacious quadrangular structure with embattled parapets and was mantled with ivy on the side fronting the demesne. The demesne was bounded on the north by the river Sullane and extends over a beautifully wooded ridge to the south and west, including a spacious deer park. Macroom parish in the barony of West Muskerry comprised nearly 10,500 statute acres. About four fifths were under tillage, the remainder being rough mountain pasture and bog. There were quarries of clay slate, which were used for building.

Macroom Castle was burnt out on 18 August 1922 following the evacuation of the British Auxiliaries, who had commanded it as a residence in 1920. Around the year 1924 Sam Williams, a prominent local Church of Ireland man, and a Roman Catholic Macroom merchant called Jeremiah O'Leary approached resident Lady Olive Ardilum to secure the castle's demesne as a recreational area for the people of Macroom. She sold the castle to the new local trustee committee for a reasonable price but reserved the site of the castle. The trusteeship still exists today. In early 1967 the main building of the castle, under the auspices of the Office of Public Works, was demolished due to concerns over the safety of the building. Mr Humprey Lynch, current chairman of the trusteeship has noted that over the ensuing years, the demolishing led to speculation about why the structure had had to be demolished in the first place. The gateway, walls and towers surrounding the castle are still intact. In the early 1970s, McEgan Secondary School/College was constructed on the site of the castle. The ninety-seven acres of the demesne are now open to the general public and boast a new nature trail that encompasses the old nineteenth-century beech avenues that led up to the main house. Macroom Golf Course also provides a recreational area with views of the River Sullane.

In terms of settlement development the owners of the castle had a huge influence. In 1750 Charles Smith observed in his *History of Cork*:

Here is a barrack for a foot barrack, and a market-house. In this town, a considerable number are employed in combining wool and spinning woollen yarn. There are here four salt pans constantly at work; they have the rock salt from England, by the way of Cork, whence it is brought by land carriage. The salt is taken by carriers from this place, into the country, where it is used in salting butter for exportation. In this town, are some whisky distillers…The Romanists have a splendid mass-house erected on an eminence at the entrance into the town, with a handsome altar, a pulpit, and a confessional chair. The houses are built of a reddish slaty rock, and there are good blue slates for covering, in the neighbourhood. [17]

In 1837 the approaches to the town centre on all sides were through a long line of cabins. Those to the west of the old bridge had been rebuilt in 'a neat and comfortable style and roofed with slate'. Macroom consisted of one principal street, nearly a mile in length. Towards

17. Smith, C., *A History of Cork* (Cork), p.181.

Macroom Castle
*c.*1900 (picture:
Humphrey Lynch).

Macroom Castle
*c.*1940 (picture:
Humphrey Lynch).

the western extremity there was a wider space in which a market house had been erected in
the early 1800s. This formed one side of a square, the opposite side of which a hotel and the
castle gateway occupied.

Samuel Lewis' account from 1837 states that there were two flour mills in operation. The
distillery and salt-works described in Smith's account have been discontinued. The principal
produce was corn, which was brought into the town daily by the farmers and purchased
by Cork merchants. The quantity sold during the year 1835 exceeded 39,000 barrels. The
market was on Saturday and was supplied with butchers' meat, vegetables and provisions at a
moderate price. From January until May there was a weekly market for pigs, many of which
are slaughtered in Macroom and afterwards sent to Cork. From May until the end of the
year, cattle fairs were held on the twelfth of every month, alternately in the town and at the
village of Masseystown, the property of Massey Hutchinson Massey, a little to the south-west
of Macroom town.

Though troops were frequently stationed in the town, there was no army barracks. Macroom
had a chief constabulary police force, for whose accommodation a handsome barrack had
been built. A manorial court for the recovery of debts not exceeding £2 was held every third

Humprey Lynch, Chairman of Macroom Castle Trustees, July 2006 (picture: K. McCarthy).

week before a judge, whose jurisdiction was comprehensive, including several parishes in addition to Macroom. The courthouse was a neat building of hewn limestone. It was ornamented with a cornice and pediment supported by two broad pilasters, between which was a handsome Venetian window with a bridewell connected with it.

In 1837 the population of Macroom was 6,137, of which 2,058 were resident in the town. The inhabitants of the town were supplied with water from springs and public pumps erected by subscription. There were no fixed sources of public amusement but the town was frequently enlivened by field sports and steeple chases, for which it was celebrated.

In Macroom in 1837 there was a rectory and vicarage and there were six acres of glebe. In 1825 the Board of First Fruits granted a loan of £1000 for the construction of St Colman's Protestant Church in Macroom. It is situated at the western end of the town, opposite the castle and close to the adjoining bridge over the Sullane. In the Roman Catholic divisions this parish was the head of a union or district and included part of the parish of Ahieragh. Macroom church was a 'handsome edifice' with a square embattled tower strengthened with buttresses and crowned with pinnacles. About 400 children were taught in the parochial school in the chapel yard, which was supported by R.H. Eyre, the incumbent of the castle, and other Protestant inhabitants. There were nine private schools, in which about 380 children were educated.

The Cork and Macroom Direct Railway made an important contribution to the development of Macroom as a key market town in County Cork. Sir John Benson, an eminent Cork City architect and engineer, initially proposed the Cork and Macroom Direct Railway. It was incorporated in 1861 and was chaired by Sir John Arnott and Joseph Ronayne. Five stations lined the thirty-seven kilometre track that cost £6,000 per mile. The line was opened on 26 May 1866 and in agreement with the Cork Bandon and South Coast Railway Company utilised the terminus at Albert Quay. In the 1870s the company built its own terminus at Summerhill South in Cork City.

In 1925 the Cork-Macroom Railway Company amalgamated with the Great Southern Railway and the Summerhill terminus closed. Trains to Macroom ran from Albert Quay. In 1929 the station buildings were acquired by the Irish Omnibus Company and eventually by CIE, who have retained the station buildings. Between 1866 and 1925 the company had 6 locomotives, over 27 coaches and over 117 wagons. The Cork-Macroom line eventually closed in 1953.

Macroom in the twenty-first century has retained its busy atmosphere. It is a colourful town with some rich architecture, such as St Colman's Protestant Church, St Colman's Catholic Church, the Castle Hotel and even more recent buildings such as the Briary Gap Theatre and Cinema. Situated in the shadow of the castle gate entrance to the square in Macroom, the local town hall can be admired as a lovely building in its own right. The decision to build a

Opening of Cork-Macroom railway line on 26 May 1866 (source: *Illustrated London News*).

Macroom town hall, est. 1901 (picture: K. McCarthy).

new town hall was taken in 1898 by the town commissioners during their first year of office. The construction contract was awarded to the Buckley Brothers from Ovens. Mrs Twomey, wife of the chairman of the town commissioners, laid the foundation stone for the new town hall in 1902. Mrs Samuel W. Baldwin officially opened the hall in 1905. However, all the traffic parked on the main street takes away from the colourfulness of the town hall and the rest of the buildings in Macroom.

3.2 The Aghinagh Way

Two roads lead from Cork to Macroom; one at the north, and another at the south side of the Lee. The comparative merits of these routes are various… that to the south enjoys a succession of those barriers, so hateful to 'Rebecca and her daughters', turnpikes-but abounds with objects of antiquarian interest; whilst the northern road is free of pikes, and holding the River Lee in view for nearly two-thirds of the distance… for several miles, it commands the valley through which the Lee pursues its tortuous course, and presents a highly varied scenery of tranquil and pastoral beauty. [18]

The country house and demesne are dominant features of the eastern section of the Lee Valley, especially as the land is fertile and workable here, compared to the ruggedness of Uíbh Laoghaire. In 1750 Charles Smith noted in his *History of Cork*:

From Iveleary, proceeding eastwards to Cork, there are several good seats and improvements in the barony… more than 200 good slate houses have been built in it; also, seven new churches and several stone bridges. [19]

The vast majority of these sites have not stood the test of time. Indeed, one could argue that in today's 'Celtic Tiger' economy a new kind of landlordism with new two-storey houses is flourishing.

The Grand Jury Map for the Macroom area in 1811 and the Ordnance Survey of 1836 show a number of large houses in the Macroom Church of Ireland parish. Mount Massey, the seat of M.H. Massey, occupied a site above the northern bank of the Sullane and was encircled by fir trees. Rockborough, the seat of T. Mitchel Brown, was situated about two miles to the west of Macroom. Sandy Hill, the residence of Thomas S. Coppinger, commanded a fine view of Macroom castle and its wooded demesne. Coolcower, the residence of W.G. Browne, was situated about a mile and a half to the south-east of the town. It still overlooks the Lee as it enters Carrigadrohid Reservoir. Firville, the residence of Philip Harding, was romantically situated at the extremity of a picturesque glen on the northern bank of the Sullane near its confluence with the Lany. Coolehane, the seat of Richard Ashe, was situated on the same bank of the river Lany. The two Codrum Houses, one the residence of Massey Warren, and the other that of Edward Ashe, were also in Macroom parish.

Unlike in John Windele's day in 1846, today there are three roads that lead from Macroom to Cork. The N22 follows the Bride Valley while the R618 and a series of third-class roads follow the course of the Lee on the northern and southern bank. The northern road (the R618) is accessed near Macroom and Harnett's Cross, which is located at the turn-off for the Gearagh and Gougane Barra. Crossing the adjacent New Bridge, signposts highlight

18. Windele, J., 1846, *Guide to the South of Ireland*, (Messrs. Bolster, Cork) p.23.

19. Smith, C., *A History of Cork* (Cork), p.194.

Ruins of Mashanaglass Castle (picture: K. McCarthy).

the nearby early nineteenth-century Bealick Mill, now a heritage centre. The R618 is windy but scenic as it makes its way eastwards through Aghinagh, Carrigadrohid, Coachford, Dripsey and Inniscarra.

The R618 provides fine views of Carrigadrohid Reservoir and also introduces the explorer to the heart of the parish of Aghinagh and the Aghinagh Way, a heritage trail that was produced by Aghinagh Heritage Group in 1999. The Way introduces a treasure trove of archaeological sites like ringforts, standing stones, wedge tombs and famine sites in areas such as Musheramore, the River Laney Valley and Ballinagree. Three different degrees of cycle tours pass through the parish of Aghinagh, using the town of Macroom as a base. Aghinagh parish is ten miles long, encompassing Mushera Mountain and the old Butter Road to the north and the River Lee and villages such as Carrigadrohid to the south.

There are many possible origins of the name Aghinagh — that it belonged to a man called Aghina, a grandson of Laoghaire, for example. Another possible meaning explaining its origin is *Ath Theinne* meaning 'ford of fire' or 'the ivy-covered field'. Within the parish is *Ard Eidhinn* Cross, which means 'heights of ivy'. Other townlands that adjoin the western bank of the reservoir consist of Ummera, or *Iomaire*, meaning 'ridge of hill'; Rosnascalp, or *Ros na Scailp*, meaning 'shrubbery of the clefts or shelters'; Coolacoosane, or *Cúl a'Chuasain*, meaning 'hillback' or 'corner of the cavern'; Coolacareen, or *Cúl a'Chairthin*, meaning 'recess of hillback of the little pillar stone'; and Caum, or *Cam*, meaning 'bend'. In fact, after a small journey northwards, the River Lee turns eastwards again, flowing towards Carrigadrohid village. A modern Catholic church, St John the Baptist's, was built here. Its windows look out over the reservoir and there are oak panels adjacent to the interior meeting room depicting the baptism of Jesus by John the Baptist.

Mashanaglass castle is a key reminder of antiquity in the parish. *Magh Sean Glas* means 'the old green plain'. The current ivy-covered ruin was built by the McCarthys and lies between Coachford and Macroom, overlooking Carrigadrohid Reservoir. Evidence — in the form of maps — indicates that there was a moated site, so the Normans may have settled here during the initial years of their invasion (*circa* 1169 onwards). However, there are written records that state that in the year 1584 the existing castle was occupied by the MacSwiney family, a professional Irish army in the employment of the McCarthys. It is believed that in 1865 a person searching for treasure or stones in the building placed a charge of gunpowder under the south-east corner, causing an explosion that did not bring him profit but caused extensive damage to the building. The ruins of Mashanaglass reveal that it was a substantial structure — four storeys high with walls that were over two metres thick. Only one floor remains — that which lies between the second and third levels. From observing its architecture one can conclude that there were at least two phases of development. In its first phase it was designed to be a typical tower house with large windows to allow as much light as possible in. The still-extant windows of the upper courses have elaborate designs (they are ogee-headed) on the side that faces out. The second phase of development includes two bastions, or projecting walls, on the lower courses of the south-west and north-east corners, which makes it clear that at a certain point in time defence became very important. Their construction involved the blocking-up of several large windows. The new bastions had small gun loops.

As part of the preparation work for the Hydro-Electric Scheme, archaeologist Edward M. Fahy excavated a horizontal mill at Mashanaglass in 1955. It was originally believed to have been a well and was known locally as *tobar an ratha*. Prior to the excavation, the site consisted of a three-walled dry stone structure with rectangular plan sides. Religious objects and personal mementoes had been affixed to the tree alongside it. During the excavation, large numbers of white pebbles were found in the sods surrounding the well. These were recorded as *'Hail Mary' stones*, as it had been customary for pilgrims to drop them in the well or leave them on the site as part of the 'rounds' at the holy well.

The water from the well was also said to cure sick babies. One of the old customs was to immerse the infants in the water. If the child turned pale or a pink colour it would die but if it turned red it would live. The excavation work also revealed that the well was in fact part of one of the most unique mills in Ireland. The date of its construction is unknown but the mill was in use up to the 1700s. A model of the mill is on display in the museum in Fitzgerald's park in Cork City. The mill has been destroyed but its ruins, as well as the holy well, can be viewed in the Mashanaglass area.

The ruins of Aghinagh parish church, Church of Ireland, are also central to the locality. It is located near the edge of the peaceful Carrigadrohid Reservoir, in the northern section of a graveyard. The church was built on the site of an earlier parish church that fell into ruin between 1615 and 1774. The contemporary rectangular nave and tower were built between 1791 and 1792 on the lands of John Bowen, the local landlord. The Bowens were originally

Aghinagh church (picture: K. McCarthy).

Aghinagh graveyard, with the high cross marking the burial place of Jeremiah O'Leary.

from Gower in Wales and one member of the family became a soldier in Cromwell's army and rose up through the ranks to Lieutenant Colonel.

A chancel was added to Aghinagh church in 1854 when the building was also re-roofed. Sections of the church were dismantled in 1889 and the building has been a ruin ever since. Elaborate stone window surrounds and tracery have survived, but the stained glass has not. The chancel contains a nineteenth-century burial plot. One can also climb to the first floor of the tower.

Enclosed by an oval-shaped stone-walled enclosure, the adjacent graveyard slopes west to east towards the reservoir. In 1970 Cork historian Richard Henchion recorded that there were at least eighty-seven graves in Aghinagh graveyard, some with expensive gravestones and others with simple designs. They are all of different dates, shapes, designs, sizes and material. Richard Henchion observes that each inscription is a miniature biography and when all are assembled together they provide close on three hundred years of condensed parish history. Catholics and Protestants lie side by side in Aghinagh graveyard. The various names on memorials remember pastors, priests, teachers, landlords, farmers, gentlemen, merchants, builders, blacksmiths and masons, to name but a few. There are some late eighteenth-century graves as well as many early nineteenth-century graves. There are also many upright slab stones that do not have any names inscribed on them. The latest burials date to the 1990s.

One major monument that catches the eye is an elaborate High cross that was built in memory of Rev. Jeremiah O'Leary. Born in 1837, he died on 23 July 1881. He was administrator of the Protestant and United parishes of Killavullen, Glenor and Wallstown and his parishioners erected the memorial. As you enter Aghinagh graveyard, the first monument on your right is a limestone cross, on which you will find a Gaelic inscription to the memory of Bishop MacEgan, Bishop of Ross, who was hanged at Carrigadroid on 11 May 1650 for his involvement in organizing troops to retaliate against Oliver Cromwell.

Bishop MacEgan of Ross was born in Duhallow and went to Spain at an early age. While on the continent he was received into the Franciscan order. Around 1630 he returned to Ireland, where he ministered to the spiritual needs of the people, principally in Munster. In due course he was promoted to many positions of importance within his order. He was a firm supporter of the war then being waged by the Confederation of Kilkenny against the English. He was also a loyal friend to Rinuccini, the Papal Nuncio, who appointed him as Chaplain General to the Ulster forces. In this capacity he was present at the Battle of Benburb on 5 June 1646, when he and his assistant chaplains heard the confessions of the officers and men, administered Communion to them and recited prayers with them before the battle.

After the battle he was deputed by Owen Roe to bring the captured banners to the Nuncio at Limerick and give a full account of the victory. He was proposed as Bishop for the See of Ross by the Nuncio himself in 1646 and, was consecrated at Waterford in March 1648. His diocese remained in Protestant hands and, since the Supreme Council had not nominated him, they were not inclined to secure any emoluments from it for him. In 1649 he was back in Munster was and still denied entry to his diocese.

When Oliver Cromwell landed in Ireland in August 1649 Bishop McEgan began a campaign to unite the country against him. He went to Kerry where he helped Colonel David Roche to raise an army to go to the relief of Clonmel, then being besieged by Cromwell. This army of about five thousand men was poorly trained and ill-equipped. At Macroom it was met by enemy forces led by the English Lord Broghill. The Irish were no match for his well-trained troops and about six hundred were killed and twenty or more taken prisoner. Among them was the bishop, McEgan. He was promised that his life would be spared if he could persuade the garrison of Carrigadrohid castle, which Broghill had bypassed the day before, to surrender. Once he arrived at the castle, McEgan dressed in his vestments and mitre. With the crosier in his hand, he addressed the garrison and told them not to surrender but to fight on for 'the faith and country'. He was seized and hanged with the reins of his own horse from a nearby tree on 11 May 1650.

Legend has it that on the night McEgan was hanged, six men — including two Dinans, two

O'Learys and two O'Riordans — took his body away from the soldiers who were guarding it and had fallen asleep. They set out for Aghinagh graveyard with the intention of burying the body there but on reaching the bridge found it guarded and so decided to travel along the southern bank in the hope of finding some place to cross the river. Suddenly a bright light shone in front of them and guided them on their way until they were opposite the graveyard, where the light crossed over the river. The men who were leading stopped when they reached the water's edge but those behind told them to go on and pushed them forward. As soon as their feet touched the water the river stopped flowing and they crossed it unhindered. After they buried the bishop they told no one where the grave was, lest the soldiers come and dig up the body.

Legend also has it that Cromwell's soldiers took the dead bishop's mitre, placed it in the window of Aghinagh church, facing the road, and stood outside the gate taking potshots at it with their muskets. Then they carved an image of the mitre on a stone and placed it in the church in mockery. In 1791, when the present building replaced the old one, it was built into the front wall of the tower where it can be seen to this day, not a mockery now but a memorial.

3.3 Fortress Carrigadrohid

We now arrive at the extremely picturesque Castle of Carrigadrohid. Like the celebrated Mause Thurm on the Rhine, its stands on a steep rock in the midst of the Lee. A Bridge on either side connects it with the banks of the river, whence the castle derives its designation, signifying the Rock of the Bridge. The Lee foams and rushes in a turbulent current around the rock on which it is built; and the spectator is impressed at once with the strength and romantic effect of its position. [20]

The small village of Carrigadrohid is located in the parish of Aghinagh and its principal buildings are Dunne's Food Store and the Spirit Store and Angler's Rest Pub. When I visited in June the new Canovee GAA pitch was flooded out. In fact, the water had risen to nearly four metres above the low-water mark for this area. On my visit I was met by two young lads, Paul Twomey and Pat Walsh, carrying water balloons meant for their friends who sat on one side of the bridge. The historic record for Carrigadrohid Bridge dates back the Civil Survey of 1656 when it recorded as a timber structure. By the early 1800s a stone bridge with six semi-circular arches had been constructed. In 1853 the bridge was swept away by a flood and replaced by the present structure.

Castles like that in Carrigadrohid were the fortified residences of local lords and chieftains, both of the native Irish families and of the descendants of the Anglo-Norman settlers. It is said Cormac McCarthy built the castle in the year 1445 to please Sabina O'Carroll, who was his bride-to-be. Castles were frequently built close to river crossings in order to control movement along and across river valleys. Carrigadrohid is unusual because it was built in the river, on a rocky island. The presence of a rock outcrop in the river made the site a natural bridging point. Relatively simple wooden structures were sufficient to span the two channels formed by the rock outcrop. However it is really when the water is low that you get to appreciate the immense engineering that went into building a castle on the bedrock. The same rock has been eroded by the river and the forces of glaciation thousands of years ago.

A modern stone plaque that explains the hanging of Bishop MacEgan in 1650 hangs on its walls. In 1703 the Hollow Sword Blade Company gained possession of the castle. In 1724 Englishman John Bowen, a former soldier, married Elizabeth Chidley Coote and moved from Kilbihane to settle at Carrigadrohid. In the early 1800s the Bowens abandoned the castle to live in their nearby new residence called Oakgrove House. The castle has been derelict for

---

20. Cody, B.A, 1859, *The River Lee, Cork and The Corkonians* (J. Barter & Sons, Cork) p.27.

Above: Carrigadrohid Dam (picture: K. McCarthy).

Right: Carrigadrohid Castle (picture: K. McCarthy).

many years and the masonry is falling apart. There are efforts to preserve the structure, because it is sad to think of the castle collapsing. It is such an imposing structure, proudly standing and promoting not only its past but the identity of the people living in the area now. Despite the fact that we cannot talk to its former residents, it is clear that a lot of human effort and emotion was put into its construction and maintenance.

Apart from the commanding presence of the castle, tucked away in a narrow part of the Lee, is Carrigadrohid Dam. The structure is another type of fortress in the area, but this time it holds back the Lee. Its counterpart is further downstream at Inniscarra. Carrigadrohid Dam was the first dam to lower its spillway gates on 23 October 1956. The length of the structure is 130 metres (120 metres shorter than Inniscarra). The height of the dam is twenty-two metres (Inniscarra is double its height). The immediate headrace has a depth of thirteen metres of water, which provides pressure and energy. Carrigadrohid's average annual output is twenty-two million kilowatts, while Inniscarra has an output of fifty-eight million kilowatts. There is a fish hatchery at Carrigadrohid where over one million salmon smolts are reared each year. These go to stock many Irish rivers and lakes, but over 100,000 are released into the Lee below the dams. They go to sea for some years but return to the Lee to spawn, sustaining the stocks in the river, both for the commercial fisherman and the anglers. The 'Borland type' fish passes in the dams ensure that the fish can move easily up and down the river.

3.4 Coachford — the Crossing of the Coach

From Carrigadrohid the river winds its way east into Inniscarra Reservoir, a large body of water just over 15 kilometres long and on average 300 metres wide. The townlands along the northern side of Inniscarra Reservoir comprise Coolnagearagh, or *Cúl an Gaorthaidh*, which means 'hill-back of the wooded glen', and Carhoo, or *Ceathramha*, which means 'quarter'.

Coachford, or *Ath an Choiste*, can be translated as 'the crossing of the coach'. This was where the Cork-Tralee mail coach crossed the Lee. A relic from this era is enshrined in nearby Rooves Bridge, which was built in the early 1950s as part of the Lee Hydro-Electric Scheme. The previous nineteenth-century structure had nine semi-circular arches and was similar to Inniscarra Bridge. On the approach road from the reservoir side is St Patrick's church. A plaque highlights that the original church on the site dates to around 1840 and that the present church was renovated in 1990. There are three high crosses in the churchyard, that of Rev. Michael Irwin (d.1943), Rev. Jeremiah Russell (d.1906) and Rev. Daniel Coakely (d. 1951). There is a memorial in the yard for Mary, 'beloved wife of John Murphy of Coolcullig, who died in February 1887'.

Coachford has a close community with a vibrant population. The village boasts many facilities, including modern shops, a GAA hall and many services usually found in bigger towns. Present-day Coachford boasts a Centra and a Gala, which is very good for such a small village space. There are also three pubs — O'Riordans, O'Callaghans and Breathnachs.

Coachford is remembered for its creamery and for its association with the Cork & Muskerry Light Railway. Known also as the Blarney Tram, the Hook and Eye, and the Muskerry Tram, it was financially successful and much used by locals. The Cork Muskerry Railway was one of the city's first narrow gauge lines. It was established with the help of the Tramways and Public Expenses (Ireland) Act of 1883, which enabled companies to obtain part or all of the finance to construct a line.

In 1883 preliminary meetings took place with prominent landowners, farmers and taxpayers to consider the possibility of establishing a light railway in the Muskerry area. On 13 October a meeting was held in the courthouse in Coachford between the interested parties and local ratepayers. The line was primarily built for tourists. It was to link Cork to the tourist town from Blarney and its historic castle. Supporters of the railway line also aimed to provide improved

Welcome to Coachford, Ath an Choiste — Crossing of the Coach (picture: K. McCarthy).

transport for locals with livestock and farm produce between the farming area north-west of Cork and the city and for coal and minerals in the reverse direction.

In the early days of planning, engineer S.G. Fraser was appointed to inspect the area. The estimated cost was £65,000. On 24 April 1884 the project was investigated by the grand jury and recommended. Work began on the construction of the railway on 4 February 1887. Robert Worthington, who was a well-known railway builder, was the contractor for the thirteen-kilometre stretch, and the contract price was £59,000. In order to finish the Blarney section in time for the autumn tourist traffic of 1884 the Blarney line was officially opened on 8 August The journey took forty minutes at a speed of 6mph on the road and 20mph through the fields. The first class return fare was one shilling and eight pence, while the third class fare was ten pence.

The Coachford section was opened on 19 March 1888. Every day, the first train for Coachford left Western Road at 8.30a.m. and the last train left at 5.30p.m. Trains left Coachford at 6.45a.m., 10.30a.m. and 4p.m. In all, the journey was 15.5 miles. In 1893 a line was opened from Coachford junction to Donoughmore. The railway line started at a terminus at Bishop's Marsh adjacent the Western Road. It was a single-storey building covered by a corrugated iron roof with a long platform. The iron engine and carriage shed spanned three tracks. The first four miles of the line going west were very like that of a tramway. From the terminus the line crossed the south channel of the River Lee in Cork City via a small bridge leading to Western Road. The initial stops were at Victoria Cross, Carrigrohane and then northwards to Leemount, Healy's Bridge and Coachford Junction.

The Cork and Muskerry Light Railway Section began at Coachford Junction and passed through Cloghroe, Gurteen, Dripsey, Kilmurray, Peake and Coachford. Due to the steep incline in the last few sections of this line, the guard used to shout 'First class passengers – hold your seats. Second class passengers – get out and walk. Third class passengers – get out and push'. The Donoughmore Extension Light Railway also began at Coachford Junction and then travelled north-west, stopping at St Ann's, Burnt Hill, Gurth, Fox's Bridge, Knockane, Firmount and Donoughmore. Passengers had to change at St Ann's for a separate line to Blarney. The first class fare was two shillings and six pence and third class was one shilling and ten pence. The first class compartment had padded seats covered in red velvet upholstery. In the third class compartment the seats were of varnished wood and ran the length of the carriage.

The station had the usual offices with a single platform, loco and goods sheds, turn table, livestock pens and two carriage sheds. The station house was built of corrugated iron with a canopy in front. There were ladies' and gents' waiting rooms. The stationmaster's office had a window with a slide facing the platform through which the tickets were sold. Whenever an important match was played in Coachford, great crowds travelled on the train. All the freight arrived by train: porter and whiskey, groceries, coal, yellow meal for Coachford and

Above: Coachford, July 2006
(picture: K. McCarthy).

Left: St Patrick's Church,
Coachford, July 2006 (picture:
K. McCarthy).

Above: Cork-Muskerry light railway line at Carrigadrohid, *c.*1900 (picture: Cork City Library).

Right: Dripsey Memorial at Ambush crossroads, marking an IRA attack against British forces on 28 January 1921 (picture: K. McCarthy).

Carrigdrohid. Pigs were carried to Cork by train for the city's bacon factory. The train was responsible for several minor accidents, especially ones involving horses. The only major incident occurred on 27 September 1927 when the 7.45a.m. train from Donoughmore collided with a steamroller. Two coaches were derailed but no one was injured.

In 1924 the line was taken over by the Great Southern Railway. In the 1920s the line began to lose passengers to the Southern Motorways Omnibus Company who began to operate buses on the Western Road. With the advent of the motor car the railway lost its popularity and passenger numbers declined. On 29 December 1934 the last train ran on the line. The Bishop's Marsh terminus was until recently occupied by Jury's Hotel. The piers of the bridge spanning the south channel of the Lee just west of Jury's Hotel are still present and in their original position though.

Following the R618 along from Coachford the townland names on to the northern bank of Inniscarra Reservoir from Roove's Bridge to Inniscarra underline the human connection with the landscape. Fergus, or *Feargus*, means 'the home of Fergus'. Feargus was a holy man and the grandson of Tighernach, who lived *circa* 600 AD. He lived with St Finbarre at his monastery at *Corcach Mor na Mumhan*, or 'the great marsh of Munster' (now the city of Cork). Cronody, or *Corra Noide* means 'stone enclosure of the church'.

Dripsey, or *An Dripseach*, can be translated as 'muddy river'. It is here that the Dripsey river joins the Lee. Dripsey Bridge is of nineteenth-century design and part of it was blown up during the Irish War of Independence in 1920. When approaching Dripsey from the Coachford side one comes to the Ambush Crossroads. An obelisk with a sculptured sword was erected here in memory of the sixth battalion. This was the first Cork brigade o the Irish Republican Army, captured while engaging British forces on 28 January 1921. They were subsequently executed in Cork Prison on 28 February 1921. Captain Jim Barrett died in Cork Prison on 22 March 1921. His comrades Timothy McCarthy, Padraig O'Mahony, Sean Lyons, Donal O'Callaghan and Thomas O'Brien are also remembered.

The tiny nearby village of Dripsey once boasted a paper mill, a cheese factory and one of the last original working woollen mills in Ireland. Samuel Lewis noted in 1837:

At the western extremity of the parish of Iniscarra are the Dripsey paper-mills, belonging to Messrs. Magnay and Co., and situated in a deep and well-wooded glen; the buildings are of handsome appearance, and the works afford employment to a number of persons, varying from 70 to 100; in the manufacture of large quantities of paper for the English market. In another part of the parish is a small stream, which turns the Cloghroe boulting-mills, which are capable, when there is a sufficient supply of water, of producing 140 sacks of flour weekly. [21]

All the above, however, are long gone. High above on the picturesquely named Carrignamuck, or rock of the pig', fifteenth-century Dripsey Castle stands guard, remembering more violent times as it watches the peaceful village. On one day in the year, little Dripsey bursts into colour, crowds and music. Flags and bunting are hung from every rooftop and telegraph pole, the local Garda sergeant directs traffic and hundreds of onlookers line the road — because this is St Patrick's Day, and for the past seven years Dripsey has been staging what it proudly claims is the shortest St Patrick's Day parade in the world, from the Lee Valley pub to The Weigh Inn pub. Further along the R618 road, one meets the townlands of Magooly, or *Magh Guala*, which means 'plain of the shoulder'. Faha, or *Faithche*, means 'lawn of green'. Gurteen, or *Goirtin*, means 'little field' and Curraleigh, or *Corra Liath*, can be translated as 'grey enclosure' or 'round-topped hill'.

---

21. Lewis, S., 1837, *Topographical Dictionary of Ireland*, (Dublin) p. 260.

3.5 *Inniscarra — Island of Friendship*

Inniscarra has a strong association with the Lee Valley and is well known by Corkonians. The area is noted for its scenery with its reservoir lake, lush green fields and the modern industrial symbols of Inniscarra Hydro-Electric Dam and the waterworks. Prior to the construction of the ESB dam, flooding downstream was an annual feature due to the topography and climate of the Cork region. In recent decades the dam has helped to curb the river, which was the primary cause of flooding. The ESB issues flood warnings to those known to be at risk downstream of the dam during periods of floods. The concrete dam at Inniscarra is of the buttress type, 250 metres long, forty-two metres high and has three spillway gates. The immediate headrace is thirty metres deep and the water provides pressure and energy. In the complex, there are two Kaplan-make turbo generators, with an output capacity of fifteen megawatts and four megawatts respectively. Hence Inniscarra can produce over fifty-five million units of electricity a year.

Inniscarra Waterworks is located two kilometres upriver from the ESB Hydro-Electric Dam. Inniscarra Lake is the biggest lake of all on the Lee. The 1960s and 1970s in County Cork were a time of industrial growth and development in the harbour area. That was acknowledged in the publication of a Cork Harbour Plan in 1972. Cork County Council's development plan of 1967 and the plan to promote the growth of satellite towns led to the need for an increased water supply. It was decided by Cork County Council, Cork Corporation and the Department of Local Government, that Inniscarra lake, with the assistance of the ESB dam, would provide the necessary volume of water needed. By 20 September 1973 the Minister for Local Government had approved the contract documents for the waterworks at Inniscarra.

An intake and pump house, built into sixteen metres of water at the edge of Inniscarra Reservoir, can withdraw water from the lake at varying levels — avoiding the intake of de-oxygenated water. The water intake tower is connected to a large pump house on the side of the valley by means of a reinforced concrete tunnel that is about forty metres long, which was blasted out of solid rock. The ESB is required by law to maintain a minimum flow in the Lee downstream at about 30 million gallons per day. The water taken from the lake is sent

Inniscarra
Dam, July 2006
(picture: K.
McCarthy).

Above: Intake pump, Inniscarra Reservoir (picture: K. McCarthy).

Left: Ruins of Inniscarra Protestant church tower (built 1756).

through a treatment process that includes settling tanks, filters and chemical treatment. Today, the Cork Harbour and City Water Scheme has a production capacity of over fifty million gallons per day.

Exploring the edge of Inniscarra Lake is a pleasure, but one does get to see the effects of the Lee Hydro Electric Scheme. In particular, field systems on the water's edge disappear into the reservoir, it is as if the area's geography and history are being erased. In early Christian times the Inniscarra area was named *Tuainn na h-Abhann*, meaning 'hillock of the river'. It was later renamed *Tuam Naofa*, or (place of) 'holy solitude'.

When Hugh O'Neill and his men rested in the area on their way to the Battle of Kinsale in 1601 O'Neill thanked the monks he stayed with for their friendship and for their hospitality and named the place *Inis Cara* or 'island of friendship'. The monk's settlement was Inishleena or *Inis Luinge*, which means 'the island of encampment'. Legend has it that St Senan set up camp *circa* 530 AD and built an abbey before going downstream to Inniscarra.

The abbey was demolished in the 1700s and the stones were used to build local houses. There is no visible trace of the old building but a new church was constructed nearby in the early 1700s. Over the western door of the tower is an inscribed plaque commemorating its erection in 1756. The adjacent graveyard is enclosed by a stone wall and is still in use. A large collection of eighteenth- and nineteenth-century headstones exists to the south of the church ruins. The earliest noted date is 1770. Just north of the ruined church are five gabled mausoleums. The largest, with near identical pedimented gables is in the section that lies furthest east. All five have been vandalised.

When Inniscarra church was first built, residents of eighteenth-century Inniscarra parish would have witnessed large herds of cattle being driven through the area en route from parts of rural Cork, Kerry and Limerick to the city's cattle markets and butcheries. A total of 90,000 animals were killed in one season alone in the year 1748. The large movement of animals led to the creation of many boreens or track ways in the countryside. The first known cattle track from Kerry to Cork passed through the southern side of the parish of Inniscarra. The trip took several days and 'standing houses' or boarding houses would be used by travelling farmers, and local fields would have been used by their cattle. In Inniscarra, local folklore has it that the cattle en route to Cork spent a night in a field at *Cnoc na Marbh* or Knocknamarriffe, the 'hill of the dead'. This was a known site of faction fighting and was located one mile from the village of Cloghroe and ten miles from Cork City. There was also a path leading to a mass rock that ran through the local fields. The path was wide enough to take a donkey and cart through. A much-used mass rock was located on the path on a secluded ditch in Bridgetstown on the side of what is locally called Looney's Lane.

Another feature of Inniscarra parish, which is highlighted in the Grand Jury Map of Cork in 1811, was the local Charter School. The Charter School system was established under a royal charter of King George II and aimed to educate Protestant and Catholic children alike. In 1748 there were forty-eight Charter Schools operating in Ireland. In addition, many poor Catholic children were taken away from parents who could not look after them, to be educated as Protestants. Boys were apprenticed to trades such as bookmaking, carpentry and farm work, while girls trained for domestic service. The Charter School at Inniscarra was in the townland of Gorteen overlooking the Lee Valley. It was a mixed school and in the year 1788 it housed twenty-six girls and fifteen boys. It was a two-storey building built of red sandstone with walls three feet thick.

Samuel Lewis, in his description of the parish in 1837, noted that a new road had been constructed to facilitate communication between this parish and the neighbouring district with the parish of Macroom. In describing the farms he stated that they 'are in general very small, and the lands were continued under tillage till they were quite exhausted; the system of agriculture, though improving, is still in a backward state; there is no bog'. A slate quarry was worked on a very limited scale. Ardrum was the seat of N. Colthurst and was situated in an extensive and wooded demesne. Cloghroe, the residence of J.C. Fitzgerald was also in the parish, while the glebe-house was the residence of Rev. W. Beresford. The glebe-house was built thanks to a gift of £100 and a loan of £1500 from the Board of First Fruits in 1816. The church was and still is on an elevated spot near the road. It was built in 1818 with a grant of £1000 from the same board.

3.6 Canovee to Farren — Toward a Pride of Place

The N22 from Macroom to Cork offers the pilgrim a view from the southern bank of the River Lee/Carrigadrohid Reservoir. In the middle of the reservoir one can see sections of what is left of two bridges from the Cork-Macroom railway line. One can be seen quite clearly in the middle of the reservoir, while the other section can be viewed from Bealahaglashin Bridge and is on the grounds of Con O'Leary's scrap yard. The river extends from the reservoir in a north-easterly direction. To follow the river you must leave the N22 and travel north on third-class roads, which are signposted as the N22 leaves the reservoir district on its route to Cork. This area is Canovee parish, called Cannaway parish in history books. *Ceann A'Mhuighe* means 'head of the plain' or it can also be *Ceanna Bhuidhe*, meaning 'yellow peaks' or 'sunny peaks'. At this point the Buingea joins the Lee. The townlands adjacent to the Lee on the southern bank all the way to Carrigdrohid Dam comprise Lehenagh, Coolnacarriga, Monallig, Bawnatemple and Killnardrish.

Lehenagh, or *Leitheanach*, means 'broad plain over the glen or river'. At the southern end are Aghthying Bridge, or *Ath Domhain* meaning 'deep ford or crossing' and Bealasheen Bridge or *Beal Aithin*, meaning 'passage of the little ford'. The Aghthying flows through the townland to join the Lee. Coolnacarriga, or *Cúl na Carrige*, means 'hill-back of the rock'. Classes, or *Clasa*, means 'hollows' or 'valleys'. Monallig, or *Moin Ailigh*, means 'rock' or 'boulder'. In recent centuries, slate quarries were worked on the northern side of the townland. Bawnatemple, or

Ruins of Cork-Macroom railway-line bridge in the Carrigadrohid Reservoir (picture: K. McCarthy).

Old Rooves Bridge, Coachford, pre-1950s flooding of the Lee Valley for the ESB Hydro-Electric Scheme (source: ESB photographic collection).

New Rooves Bridge, Coachford, being constructed in preparation for the flooding of the Lee Valley for the ESB Hydro-Electric Scheme (source: ESB photographic collection).

Rooves Bridge 2006 (picture: K. McCarthy).

Rooves ringfort (picture: K. McCarthy).

Overgrown ruins of Aglish churches (picture: K. McCarthy).

Badhún An Teampaill, means 'enclosure of the church'. An ancient church was erected in the area and was reputed to be one of the largest early monastic enclosures in Munster. In 1817 a Protestant church opened near the older church and this is also a ruin amidst a surrounding graveyard. Killnardrish, or *Cill an Ard Dorais*, can be translated as 'church of the high door'. In the Civil Survey of Muskerry in 1640 it was noted that another parochial church was located in this townland near the bank of the Lee.

Leaving Carrigadrohid and following the southern bank towards Rooves Bridge and Coachford, one cannot but admire the pillars of Nettleville Estate, once the home of R. Neville Nettles. In 1837 Samuel Lewis noted that the other principal gentry houses in Canovee parish were Killinardrish House, the residence of R. Crooke; Llandangan House, that of S. Penrose; Lieutenant Col. White's Rockbridge Cottage; T. Gollock's Forest House; J. Bowen's Oakgrove; W. Furlong's Coolalta and an elegant Italian styled lodge that was the home of R. J. O'Donoghue.

There is another memorial in this region, one for the poorer classes: further east on the road you come to Soup Kitchen Cross Roads. A memorial was erected here in 1998 by Canovee Historical Society to remember Ireland's Great Famine and the efforts made to provide relief to residents in Canovee parish. Continuing eastwards, the road travels alongside the Kame River as it enters Inniscarra Reservoir. Rooves Bridge provides access across the reservoir to Coachford. Rooves Mór and Rooves Beg are two large townlands. Rooves, or *Ruaidhtibh*, can be translated as 'reddish spots of land'. I was intrigued to see so many archaeological features associated with past settlements in the area on the Ordnance Survey. I was even more surprised and impressed to find out that the majority of them had been well preserved by the local population.

The archaeological monuments all date from different centuries, with features such as Bronze Age cooking sites, or *fulacht fia*, in abundance, as well as several ringforts, church ruins, old farm houses and holy wells. A cross-section from Rooves' history is represented, with a wealth of features to explore. On my first visit I came across a very well-preserved and cared for well house on the roadside. I soon discovered from the nearby house that it was local farmer Finbarr Crowley who had such pride in the area. Finbarr has a passion for Irish and

Above: 'Caretaker' Finbarr
Crowley at Rooves Holy
Well (picture: K. McCarthy).

Left: Site of St Finbarre's
Chuch at Cill na Cluaine,
note the low mound near the
horse (picture: K. McCarthy).

local archaeology and history. His passion is fuelled by the presence of a ringfort, stone row
and holy well on his land. On my tour of the local area with Finbarr he pointed out that his
sites are among thousands in Ireland, but the sites on his land are as important as the rest in
promoting local identity. He observes that the sites should be preserved for generations to
come: 'They have been here for a long time. We should be honoured to have them on our
land. You can work around these monuments — you can incorporate the past and present
successfully. We should mind what has been left behind.'

Finbarr Crowley's ringfort stands 150 metres above sea level, is approximately 30 metres in
diameter and provides panoramic views of the area. There are four other ringforts visible to

the east, west and south. Ringforts are early Christian farmsteads and like modern farms are corralled spaces. Finbarr himself discovered a souterain to the north of the fort. An exploration by UCC Archaeological Services revealed two chambers/passages, both one metre in height and containing a calf bone and the base of a furnace for smelting iron. The iron had some lime incorporated into it, which reduced the required temperature for the smelting process. The addition of lime to the process is a medieval technique. Finbarre's theory for the underground chamber is that it was a refuge in times of attack. In addition, Finbarre was quick to note that, 'Many farmers have the idea that "archaeological people" will come out, put a barrier around your land and not give access to farmers. Archaeologists do not do that. They give advice on how to preserve sites…in the majority of cases, they do not have money to excavate every site they encounter'.

Finbarre's stone row is one of six pairs of stones extending in a semi-circle in the immediate area. These stones are all large, on average three metres in height. They are the nearest stone alignments to Cork City. Finbarr observed that because of the overall semi-circle shape occupied by the six pairs of stone rows, they must have had some sort of ritual function. There are also *fulacht fia*, or Bronze Age cooking sites in Finbarre's townland. Those sites for the most part have only been discovered when fields were ploughed up and burnt and broken up stones are revealed.

Finbarr Crowley has a major passion for Our Lady's Holy Well, which is located on his land. He deems himself the caretaker of the monument just like his grandfather, Dan Collins, before him. In recent decades Finbarr has maintained the well house and its surrounds, making it a visible and sacred site. The well is for the people of the locality. It is a place for local people to come and pray and to pay their respects. The well is located at a cross-section of three parishes: Canovee, Ovens and Aghabullogue. Finbarr supplies 'visiting statues' each month, as well as night-lights to put on display in the well house. Mass is held at the site every August. Finbarr encourages local people to bring night-lights and to light them in small glasses at the well.

Doing 'the rounds' involving walking around the well house clockwise and comprised saying seven sets of seven 'Our Fathers', seven 'Hail Marys' and seven 'Glory Bes'. After the seven sets, one drinks the water from the well and blesses oneself. One then makes seven crosses on the side of the well and ties a piece of cloth on a whitethorn tree. Whatever ailment one has is supposed to blow away with the cloth on the tree. No one touches the cloth for fear of getting the ailment. The rounds are completed over three days on a Sunday and again on the following Friday and Sunday. Extra powers were granted on Palm Sunday, Good Friday and Easter Sunday. In particular, the well is said to cure toothaches and headaches.

One of the legends attached to the well is that St Olan from Aghabullogue gave tuition to St Finbarre at the well as he walked down the Lee. Another legend is that the water of the well does not boil. When I asked Finbarr if he ever tested this, he was quick to note that 'it is tradition' and that he accepts the well's powers. Mass has also been said at Rooves Well since penal times and the tradition is carried on today. A specially created mass rock was moved near the well in the year 2000.

Very few regions in County Cork have a holy well that is in good condition, but in Aglish parish, which is adjacent, there is another well-kept well dedicated to Our Lady. Seven kilometres to the east of Rooves, in the townland of Walshestown, Derry Hurley is the 'caretaker', just like his father. Mass is said in the month of May. Stone relics from Inisluinge Abbey from the Inniscarra side are on display in the well. The water from the well is said to cure earaches.

Aglish means *Eaglais* or 'church'. There are remains of three medieval churches within four miles of Aglish. Near Aglish Cross Roads there are remains of two ancient church ruins. They are built at right angles to each other and overlook Farren Woods. The older is aligned to the north-south, and the younger one is aligned in a west-east direction. The older building is the same size as Macloneigh church — nearly twenty-five metres long and ten metres wide. The gable walls are all overgrown and large sections have been reduced to just a mound. Within the interior of the older church is a tomb that dates back to 1795. Both churches are simply named Aglish. In the associated graveyard there is a section for famine victims, with stone stumps protruding from the ground.

The third church is St Finbarre's Church and it is located three kilometres to the east, near the reservoir bank in the townland of Ballineadaig, or *Baile an Eadaigh*, meaning 'Eady's habitation'. It might also read *Baile an Eadaigh*, meaning 'place of the cloth or clothing'. The church is called *Cill na Cluaine* meaning 'church of the meadow'. This was one of the places where St Finbarre is reputed to have died in the year 623 AD. Cloyne in East Cork is also reputed to be the place of his death. The *Cill na Cluaine* complex has all the hallmarks of being a monastic enclosure. Today, a low circular mound of earth encloses the low rectangular mound of a church. In the adjacent lands is a farmhouse, which is from the early 1800s and was once the hunting lodge of the Parker family. Today, it is the residence of the fifth generation of the Lehane family.

The townland of Farren, or *Fearann na Seisrighe*, means 'land of the plough team' and comprises approximately 1,000 acres. Farran Woods overlooks the impressive Inniscarra Lake/Reservoir. During my fieldwork on a summer's day in June, two children were playing on the swings and slides, supervised by their grandparents. A larger group were having a barbeque. Several names were carved into the picnic tables. A dingy floated aimlessly in Inniscarra Lake. A father and his two sons were fishing. Something tugged at the father's fishing line. An eel was caught and the father was dismayed, but one of the sons piped up with 'well done dad'. He was a hero and this was an amazing adventure. This is the great Farren Wood on the southern bank of the Lee, located just north of Aglish. Farren, like Gougane Barra, is another of Cork's sacred sites and it abounds with opportunities to engage in traditional family activities.

Apart from the forest paths through the woods, one can also explore Inniscarra Lake. This is one of the two lowland lakes that were created by the Electricity Supply Board in 1956 and it spans an area of over 530 hectares. Although not all of it is fishable there are over twenty-five miles of bank side. Both Inniscarra and Carrigadrohid Lakes form an integral part of the River Lee system. The Lee is renowned for having some of the best fishing in Ireland. Inniscarra Lake is suitable for coarse angling, with its gently sloping banks and appropriate water depths. Salmon, trout and pike are also plentiful. A licence for coarse fishing is not necessary and there is no closed season. Permits can be obtained for a small fee from the ESB office in Inniscarra or the ESB shop in Macroom. Permission may also be required in order to cross certain landowners' property. The South Western Regional Fisheries Board introduced 200 adult bream into the upper Carrigadrohid Lake in 1974. It was in 1989 that large stocks of bream were discovered in the lower Inniscarra Lake. Today excellent shoals exist throughout Inniscarra.

Rudd are abundant and usually found with the bream in Iniscarra lake. Large shoals of small rudd are often found at recommended areas. Bream-rudd hybrids are also found in Inniscarra Lake, where specimens weighing over three pounds have been caught. Hybrids are usually located with the bream and at the deeper water in Oakgrove. Quality salmon-fishing is concentrated on the nine-mile stretch downstream of the Inniscarra Dam. Spring fish enter the Lee early in February. However, it is March before they regularly arrive at Inniscarra. April and May are peak months for spring salmon. The open season for salmon angling is from 1 February to 30 September. The River Lee is also fairly well stocked with brown trout. Inniscarra Lake is also good for watersports like waterskiing. The Water Ski Centre on Inniscarra Lake is open all summer from May to September, and welcomes visitors. A large new boating complex has been built on Farren lake and it protrudes into the lake, changing the lake landscape.

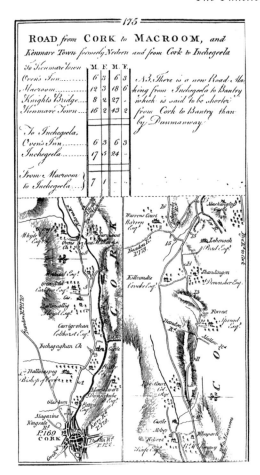

Taylor and Skinner's *Road Map* of the Ballincollig area, 1779 (source: Cork City Library).

3.7 *Ballincollig — Home of the Royal Gunpowder Mills*

In recent years Ballincollig, a settlement on the southern side of the Lee Valley, has grown considerably in size, both in terms of population and number of houses. The village has expanded in accordance with the needs of its resident and the commuter population. The functions of Ballincollig have changed over time, and they have ranged from providing defence — with Ballincollig Castle on the Anglo-Norman Irish frontier in the fourteenth century — through to providing houses and shops in the nineteenth century for workers in the gunpowder mills. Ballincollig also helped to create and develop a satellite town with a population of over 20,000 people in recent decades.

Archaeological excavations on the Ballincollig Bypass in 2002/2003 uncovered habitation sites (houses and *fulacht fia*) from prehistory and traces left by Ballincollig's first settlers 5,000 years ago. Finds from the Neolithic era or Late Stone Age Ireland include a house that was excavated during the construction of the bypass at Ballinaspig More (*circa* 3900–*circa* 3600 BC), as well as a nearby ritual pit at Carrigrohane in which pottery, beaker pottery, flint fragments, charcoal and charred seed were discovered. From the late Neolithic and Bronze Age, fifteen *fulacht fia* were excavated (*circa* 2500 BC). A Bronze Age to Late Bronze Age house (*circa*1500 BC) was excavated during the construction of the bypass at Ballinaspig More, and cremation pits were found at Barnagore (2100 BC) and at Carrigrohane (*circa* 1500 BC). An Iron Age house was also excavated during the construction at Ballinaspig More (340 BC). Two conjoined enclosures from the Early Medieval era were found during the construction of the bypass at Curaheen. A house foundation was also discovered, as well as an enclosure and associated finds (dating to *circa* 700 AD).

In the course of eight weeks during the spring of 2006 the excavation of a ringfort/enclosure at Carrigrohane, Ballincollig took place to make way for Cork County Council's new Fire Department headquarters, located adjacent to the enclosure. The enclosure/ringfort inspired the architect to design the new headquarters in keeping with the archaeological site. Most of the land (1.99 acres) adjacent to the proposed location for the new Fire Department headquarters was covered by a trivallate enclosure/ringfort. The monument is protected by the National Monuments Legislation and was excavated by Dan Noonan Archaeological Services. The ditches and exterior were excavated, exposing two deep ditches and exterior features in the form of a post holes for wall supports for a house and an underground chamber.

A few years ago on a flight over the then-undeveloped fields at Carrigrohane, Dr Daphne Pochin Mould, a well-known and respected aerial photographer, pilot and archaeologist who lives nearby, discovered the shape of the enclosure's banks and ditches through crop marks. Cork County Council's Archaeologist, Catryn Power, commented that the excavation of the ringfort and the promotion of our archaeological heritage was, and is, an integral part of the council's work. Archaeology was brought to life for the community.

Nearby is Ballincollig castle, which was built in the early 1300s (AD) and was the castle of the Colls, an Anglo-Norman family — hence the name Ballincollig, or *Baile an Chollaigh*. The castle was handed over to the Barrett family, a Norman clan in the barony of East Muskerry after whom the barony, which includes Ballincollig, is named. The Barretts had allegiances with local Irish families. The castle was destroyed in 1641, and in 1689 it was garrisoned by troops of Catholic King James II. In 1659 the manor of Ballincollig castle had eighteen inhabitants. The castle was a ruin until some renovations by the local landlord, Thomas Wise, in the nineteenth century. Sine then, the castle has fallen into disrepair.

Ballincollig continued to be a small community until 1794, when Charles Henry Leslie, a leading Cork merchant, established the local gunpowder mills — a unique industrial complex in southern Ireland. Shortly after, Leslie built his residence, Oriel House. Increased concern about the security of the gunpowder mills, coupled with the British government's policy of creating a monopoly of gunpowder manufacture in these islands, greatly influenced the Board of Ordnance's decision to buy out Leslie in 1805. In March 1805 the board appointed its chief clerk of works for powder mills, Charles Wilkes, as superintendent of the Ballincollig Gunpowder Mills. Wilkes began by improving access to the complex from the old Killarney road to the north, by entirely rebuilding Inniscarra Bridge, replacing the six arches that were there (original date of construction unknown) with twelve semi circular arches. The area of the barracks and mills, including administration buildings, a network of canals and the new cavalry barracks, was greatly expanded in the 1806-1815 period, and the greater part of those 431 acres was enclosed behind a high stone wall.

In 1810 the Army barracks were built in town to house soldiers who would protect the gunpowder. The outer perimeter stone walls extended from the eastern gate of the mills to Inniscarra Bridge. Ballincollig barracks was located to the north of Main Street in Ballincollig town centre. In 1837 the army barracks could accommodate eighteen officers and 242 non-commissioned officers and privates. In the centre of the quadrangle there were eight gunsheds and near them there were stables and offices. Within the walls was a large and commodious schoolroom. The police depot for the province of Munster was situated here and the men here were drilled until they were efficient and then drafted to different stations in the province.

The interior of the barracks was significantly remodelled in the mid-nineteenth century, particularly during the Crimean War in the 1850s. The barrack square, officers' mess and stables were built between 1875 and 1922 and were set back from the road behind the high stone wall. The old carriage store is now used by O'Flynn Construction as a marketing suite for the Ballincollig Town Centre development. This carriage store has recently been fully restored to its original state, exposing the beautiful limestone walls and natural slate roof.

In 1834 the Board of Ordnance sold the gunpowder mills to the Tobins, a Liverpool family. In the same year, Thomas Tobin married Catherine Eillis and in 1835 they moved into Charles Henry Leslie's former house. Catherine was an avid painter so Thomas built an oriel, or a recess with a polygonal window, built out from a wall. From this time on the house became affectionately known as Oriel House. The mills had lain derelict for twenty years before that.

Around the year 1860 approximately 500 people were employed in the gunpowder mills. Two of the raw materials needed for the gunpowder were imported: sulphur from Sicily and saltpetre from India. The third ingredient, charcoal, was produced locally. The Lee provided the power to turn the waterwheels for grinding the raw materials and manufacturing the gunpowder. Most of the finished product was exported to Liverpool before it was sent onto to Africa.

Thomas Tobin died in 1881 and was buried in Inniscarra. After Thomas Tobin's death Lady Catherine moved to Albert House Mansion in London. The house passed through a series of owners: Colonel W. Balfe (1886), J. McKenzie MacMorron (1893), Lt. Col. Onslow (1911) and W.J.O. O'Hara (1916). In 1916 the house was set on fire by Republicans, but local people cut the roof joyces and saved the eastern part of the house. In the early twentieth century there were a number of other residents — A.F. MacMullen (1938) and Maire Louise Perrins (1947). In 1970 Bill Shanahan bought the house and he officially opened it as a hotel in 1983. In recent years the hotel has undergone renovations and extensions. What is heartening to see is that many of the function rooms are named after key residents of the house, such as Thomas Tobin.

As for the mills, in 1888 they were bought by John Briscoe and soon came under the control of Curtis's and Harveys. The mills closed in 1903 due to the advent of the production of dynamite. The Curtis's and Harvey's mills were then absorbed into Imperial Chemical Industries (ICI). The site was bought by Cork County Council in 1974 and developed into a public park.

In 2002 the draft County Development Plan designated the complex of the ruins of the gunpowder mills as a Protected Structure. A number of structures within the complex were recognised by Cork City Council as having significant heritage/archaeological and architectural merit and were restored. The gunpowder mills are now in disrepair but the area is still open for walks and exploration. In addition, a new book on the history and geography of the Ballincollig Gunpowder Mills by Ballincollig locals Jenny Webb and Anne Donaldson was published by Nonsuch Ireland in 2006.

With the creation and blossoming of the Ballincollig Gunpowder Mills came a need for housing and community services. The first church in Ballincollig was built in 1808 and is now the local community hall. The old church was replaced in 1866 with the Church of St Mary and St John, during the tenure of Canon David Horgan PP. The 1866 church was built by Barry McMullen and designed by George Goldie. The site belonged to Thomas Wise, who allowed his quarry to be used free of charge for stones at Coolroe.

In the 1860s there were 875 inhabitants in Ballincollig, with a large number of British soldiers with their families living in the town. By 1900 an elaborate social structure was in place, comprising military, police, clergy, teachers, shop-owners, vintners and landowners. Between 1948 and 1955 Cork County Council purchased land and developed four local authority housing schemes at Ballincollig and Carrigrohane — three housing schemes were

Tour with Jenny Webb and Anne Donaldson, Ballincollig Gunpowder Mills, January 2006.

Oriel House, now
a key hotel in
Ballincollig (picture:
K. McCarthy).

Ballincollig Shopping
Centre, opened in
2005 (picture: K.
McCarthy).

completed in the vicinity of the East Gate viz. Leo Murphy Terrace, Fr Sexton Park and Peter O'Donovan Crescent (early 1960s development).

The main source of employment during the early twentieth century were the gravel pits of John A. Wood and O'Regan's Poulavone, as well as the military. These all contributed to the local economy. In 1956 Ballincollig graveyard was built. Between 1960 and 2006 an extensive number of housing units were created and the village turned into a small town. In 2006 the population stood at 20,000, with a town centre, the newest feature of which is historic but still a good example of what is happening to modern towns and villages in Ireland.

Today Ballincollig is home to a very family-orientated community with four primary schools and two secondary schools. There are many sports clubs in the town. These include Ballincollig Rugby Club, Ballincollig GAA and Ballincollig Soccer Club. Two Catholic churches are located in the town. The modern Christ Our Light Church is located on the west side of the town, while the old St Mary and St John's Church is located near the centre of the town on Station Road. Other religious groups also hold services at various locations in Ballincollig. Among the other amenities located in Ballincollig are a library, a multiplex cinema, playgrounds, three shopping centres and the Ballincollig Regional Park. A new shopping centre opened in October 2005 and the housing estates continue to be built on the southern side of the Lee Valley.

3.8 Fragments of Antiquity — Currykippane and J.J. Collins

On a beautiful lookout on the northern side of the Lee Valley, near Cork and overlooking the approach of the river to the Lee Fields, stands the jagged ruin of Currykippane, which gives its name to the surrounding burial ground. Writers differ in opinion about the origin of the place name. Many explain it as *Coradh-Ceapchain*, Currykippane, or 'homestead of the little clearance'. In the distant past a dense wood crowned the hillside on which a clearance for a church or dwelling would be necessary. Other accounts attribute 'Cora' to the weir or ford that formerly crossed the river at the foot of the hill, and served as an approach to the *ceapchain* or 'little clearance'. In fact, it is told that during Ireland's penal days the priest waited in secret at Clogheen Calvary site to meet funerals on their way to Curraghkippane. The funeral cortege would stop and the priest would recite prayers for the dead.

Of the church called 'Corkapan' in 1291 AD, little is known. Obviously, it was founded during a much earlier period and belongs to a group of smaller pre-Reformation churches and associated internments. Currykippane appears to have been restricted to families (and their descendants) who had long resided in the neighbourhood. The building appears to have needed repairs in the 1600s and is reputed to have been abandoned by 1693. In 1860 only the eastern gable, some fragments of the south wall, and part of the west gable remained. The form of the perpendicular window

Clogheen Cross and Crucifixion Memorial (picture: K. McCarthy).

Central remains of Curraghkippane church (picture: K. McCarthy).

in the chancel, as well as the stone credence in a niche in the eastern wall and a piscina in the south wall, highlight the date of the church.

Today the fragmentary remains of the rectangular church exist — only fragments of its north and south walls survive. The west wall is now featureless and ivy-clad. The eastern wall stands tall with a narrow central window ope. The interior of the church is now crowded with burials, some recent. The earliest noted inscribed headstones in Currykippane date to 1794. There is a large famine burial pit in the eastern part of the graveyard. Outside the south-eastern corner of a Jewish burial ground can be seen.

Apart from its antiquarian interest, Currykippane is revered by Corkmen as the resting place of Jerome J. Collins, a distinguished scientist and journalist. From a sketch of his life that appeared in *The Celtic Magazine* soon after his death, we learn that he was born at Cork in 1841. His father, Mark Collins, was a merchant and manufacturer in the city and a member of the town council for twenty-two years. At the age of sixteen young Collins became a pupil of Sir John Benson, then City and Harbour Engineer. Collins soon became assistant engineer and was in charge of important works in the river and harbour, notably the erection of North Gate Bridge. On emigrating to America he worked on several important municipal works and became Street Commissioner of Hudson City in 1869.

The possibilities of a general 'weather service' had a fascination for him, and owing to his articles on the subject he became attached to the editorial staff of the *New York Herald*. His idea was to make collected information about the weather useful in a practical way, and after careful experiments extending over an entire year, he began sending his famous storm predictions for the *Herald* to Europe. Notwithstanding criticism of the English press, he persevered and organized a weather bureau. In 1878 Jerome Collins attended the Meteorological Congress in Paris, where he received high honours and contributed two papers on storm warnings.

When Cordon Dennett organized an expedition to the North Pole, Jerome Collins became attached to the exploring party as scientist and correspondent. The *Jeannette*, a steamer acquired from the British government, left San Francisco on 9 July 1879. His last communication, dated 27 August 1879 from Bering Strait closed worryingly:

All before us now is uncertainty, because, our movements will be governed by Circumstances over which we have-no control. We are amply supplied with fur clothing and provisions, so that we can feed and keep warm in any event for some time. Our dogs will enable us to make exploration a considerable distance from the ship. Feeling that we have the sympathy of all we leave at home, we can go forth, trusting in God's protection and our good fortune. —Farewell!

Jerome Collins (source: Cork City Library).

In June 1851 the *Jeannette* was abandoned in the icepack in northern latitudes. Two boats, however, were sound, and they were used to look for land and food. During a storm one boat and its crew became separated from the other and both got lost. Collins, with the captain and others, landed in a desolate region where they endured great deprivation. A small party went in search of food and failed to return. Meantime, while awaiting an opportunity for a further expedition, the party became exhausted and died of starvation. Commander DeLong was the last survivor. His diary entry dated 30 October 1881 stated that Collins was dying by his side.

Three of the party, who lost their way while looking for food, reached Siberia, from where a message was sent to the United States government. A search party was immediately dispatched from New York and after a long and hazardous search the bodies of the others were recovered. On 8 March 1884 the remains of Jerome J. Collins landed at Queenstown so they could be buried in Currykippane graveyard. The funeral procession, which passed through the streets of Cork during terrible weather, was long remembered.

3.9 Carrigrohane - A Geography Inspired

From Ballincollig, the Lee meanders towards the tidal water. Its journey is nearly over. On one side of the valley is Curraghkippane and on the other, soaring above the scene just before one encounters the Carrigrohane Straight Road, is Carrigrohane Castle. Carrigrohane translated means *Carraig Raitheach* or 'the rock of the ferns'. The second translation is *Carraig Rothain* or 'the rock of the (hangman's) noose'.

Here, the geography of a place is, again, as important as its history. The development of Carrigrohane castle from its origins to the present day was inspired by its geographic location, so close to a cliff face and overlooking the Lee and one of the principal approach roads leading

Nathaniel
Grogan's sketch of
Carrigrohane Castle
*c.*1800 (courtesy:
Crawford Municipal
Art Gallery).

into Cork. In fact, its walls overlook Hell Hole — a favourite swimming and fishing haunt for
many centuries that is near the present-day Angler's Rest Pub.

The development of the site began around the year 1180 when King Henry II granted Milo
De Cogan, an Anglo-Norman lord, several hundred acres of land south and west of the walled
town of Cork. In 1207 Richard DeCogan, a relative, was given the manor of Carrigrohane
and his successors built a castle. In 1464, on the occasion of a new charter granted to the city
of Cork, the western limits of the liberties of the city were extended to Carrigrohane castle.
In 1317 William Barrett, in consequence of his father Robert working with the king's armies
against 'the King's enemies', was granted two parts of the local land of 'Gronagh' and the castle
on that land. By the 1400s, the DeCogans of Carrigaline returned as overlords of the Barrett
property. In the 1500s, the castle supported the Irish Earl of Desmond in his revolt against
the English crown. When the Earl of Desmond's uprising failed, the Queen's Lord Deputy
(in around 1600) gave the lease of Carrigrohane to Sir Richard Grenville, on the condition
that he would repair the ruined walls of the castle and build a new house. Subsequently, the
lands were given to Sir William St Leger. The new house could be described as a Tudor castle
– a type of semi-fortified mansion with three storeys lit by four windows on each storey. The
medieval castle has partly survived next to the present-day dwelling.

The builders of fortified houses were concerned with creating a formal plan based on
renaissance lines in order to accommodate more luxurious living standards. Fortified houses
were symmetrical and had a central doorway. The structures resembled semi-defended country
houses, with many of the features found in earlier castle conceptions, such as crennelations,
mural stairs and bawn walls, all being abandoned. Today, there are twenty-two fortified houses
in Cork that have survived the test of time.

Around 1601 the house and lands through Warham were granted to Abraham Baker and
Barrachias Baker. In the 1640s, during the Confederate War, Lord Inchiquin occupied the
dwelling and large portions of the interior were dismantled. The site became the haunt of a
man called Cope, who terrorised and robbed the countryside with his gang.

In the ensuing years, the Baker family returned and the house was rebuilt. One of the sons,
John, had a niece who married Peter Wallis. Their son John died in 1731 and the property
passed to his brother, Barrachias of Ballycrenane in Cloyne. His daughter Clotilda married Sir
Edward Hoare in 1771. The Hoares were a Cromwellian family. The house was reduced to a

Right: Carrigrohane Castle, July 2006 (picture: K. McCarthy).

Below: Carrigrohane Castle 2006 (picture: K. McCarthy).

ruin again as the family squandered their fortune and were forced to abandon the structure.

Around the year 1790 Nathaniel Grogan, a Cork painter, depicted the house gloomily with all its contours, located on its cliffside overlooking what look like flour mills in the foreground and two gentlemen fishing in the Lee. In 1837 Samuel Lewis referred to those mills and others in the vicinity when he noted that they were capable of manufacturing between 350 and 400 sacks of flour weekly. Around the year 1830 Carrigrohane castle passed to Augustus Robert McSwiney, a corn merchant in the city (at 18 Dunbar Street) who also owned Carrigrohane Flour Mills, mills that are illustrated in Grogan's painting. McSwiney is reputed to have worked with Cork architects Deane and Woodward to carry out extensive reconstructions. One of the key features especially commissioned on the occasion was a chimney mantle piece emblazoned with the shields of the McSwiney family. During this time the Carrigrohane Straight Road, a two-and-a-half mile stretch of a new line of road from Cork, was constructed to replace the old road.

St Peter's Church, Carrigrohane (picture: K. McCarthy).

Soon the McSwiney family ran out of money for refurbishment and in 1846 the Hoares bought the property back and lived there until the 1940s. In 1946 the house was bought by Mr Burnett and in 1976 it was purchased by Leo and Mary O'Brien. In 1989 Cork County Council, following the collapse of the cliff face onto the roadway, demolished the northern half of the remaining medieval castle. Today, the house is a splendid building retaining all of its charm and identity. Its owners, the O'Brien family, have ensured that the legacy of this historic building can be used in the modern world. As well as that, its long history has been remembered and commemorated in a wealth of papers and books by scholars like James N. Healy, and painters like Nathaniel Grogan.

Near Carrigrohane castle is the imposing limestone structure of St Peter's Church, which was originally built in the seventeenth century as a Protestant church. Samuel Lewis in 1837 described it as a 'small plain edifice' that had been repaired in the 1830s. Several changes were witnessed in the ensuing decades.

In 1851 the chancel, west end, tower and spire were erected under Rev. Hodder. A contribution by Thomas Tobin, owner of the Royal Gunpowder Mill, financed the installation of the stained glass windows in the chancel in memory of his only son, Arthur Lionel, who was killed in India. The annex to the church was built under Rev. Robert S. Gregg to the design of William Burges, architect of St Finbarre's cathedral. Gregg's father was John Gregg, Bishop of Cork, who was responsible for raising the money to build the cathedral in the late 1800s. The design for the cut stone spire is by W.H. Hill of Cork and his work replaced an earlier one (of timber and slate) in 1896-1897.

The graveyard is a mixed Protestant and Roman Catholic graveyard. Most of the earlier gravestones are either limestone or sandstone, but some of the new gravestones are in marble. There are very few tombs or monuments, with the main exception being the Murphy family vault (of the Murphy brewery fame). There are also associations with Cork City as several business families are buried there — such as the Bass family (solicitors), Rohus (furriers) and Dunscombes (merchants). The earliest gravestone dates to 1735. There are other eighteenth-century gravestones, but most of the gravestones are from the nineteenth and twentieth centuries.

3.10 Lee Fields — Journey's End

The Lee Fields extend from the County Hall for just over two and a half miles. The weir provides a boundary of the river's fresh water and tidal water. It is here that the die-hards swim in the Lee all year in all weathers, where people walk their dogs, where fitness fanatics jog and stretch, couples discuss the day's challenges and people watch the waters flow. It is here that the Lee splits into two, creating a north and south channel, both of which flow around the city centre islands. One can see the northern channel as it struggles to carve a path for itself, while the south channel flows on with ease. St Finbarre's cathedral overlooks the southern channel and declares the journey's end and a new beginning for Cork's patron saint.

(I) UTILISING THE PULSE — CORK CITY WATERWORKS:

The pulse and power of the river was once used in the Cork City Waterworks. The buildings, which stand at the waterworks site today, date from the 1800s and 1900s, but water has been supplied to the city of Cork from the site since the 1760s. A foundation stone today commemorates the building of the first pump-house, which was itself constructed on the Lee road in the late eighteenth century. It was in 1768 that a Nicholas Fitton was elected to carry out the construction work needed for the new water supply plan. The waterwheel and pump sent the river water unfiltered to an open reservoir called the 'City Basin', which was located above the Lee road. This water was then pumped from here to the city centre through wooden pipes.

Between the years 1856 and 1857 the corporation obtained a sanction from the parliamentary treasury to acquire a loan of £20,000 to upgrade the Lee Road waterworks. In February 1857 John Benson's plan for a new waterworks was given to several eminent engineers in London for consultation, and the project progressed. During 2004 and 2005 the old waterworks building went through a renovation programme.

Officially opened in October 2005, the site of the old waterworks is now known as the Lifetime Lab, a Cork City Council initiative funded by EFTA, or the European Free Trade Association. The development of Lifetime Lab involved the conservation and restoration of the old waterworks site, all under the watchful eye of Jack Coughlan and Associates, industrial archaeologist Dr Colin Rynne, and Imagination Ltd. The former engine rooms are now used to house the exhibition, while the former coal store houses the conference theatre and meeting room and the former boiler house is now the main reception area for Lifetime Lab. The engines and boilers are still in the buildings today. The Lifetime Lab Information Centre is open to all visitors, particularly class groups, and aims to provide information on different environmental topics, including energy, waste and water. (Visit www.lifetimelab.ie for more details).

(II) COUNTY HALL — A SKYSCRAPER TO CATCH THE EYE:

Along with Cork's nineteenth-century transformation in the areas of infrastructure (roads, bridges, waterworks) education and culture, local politics also changed. For centuries the only semi-government body that operated outside the municipal corporations was the grand jury, which was introduced by the Normans in the late twelfth century. The term 'county' was also introduced by the Normans as part of the duties of a sheriff of a county, who was to collect the king's revenue within that county. For centuries, the grand juries had a judicial function that varied from area to area, depending on what kind of Gaelic Irish presence there was. However, by the seventeenth century the grand juries took on an administrative role, dealing not only with taxes but also with law and order, the building of roads, bridges, and gaols, as well as poor relief.

The Local Government (Ireland) Bill of 1898 aspired to reform the government of Ireland's counties. The introduction of a County Council would take over the administration and taxation duties of the grand juries at County Sessions. The Councils would nominate the Board of Governors of the District Lunatic Asylums, and also take over the responsibilities and duties of the rural sanitary authorities. Many leading figures in Ireland saw the Act as an attempt to kill the struggle for Home Rule with kindness.

A County Council was established in each administrative county. The members of the new council were elected in county electoral divisions. The Council also comprised the chairmen of rural district councils. All the councils were to be elected by parliamentary electors plus peers and women. The parliamentary electors at this time were property owners — occupiers of property who paid rates directly or through the landlord as an addition to rent and any lodgers who paid more than £10 on rent per annum.

In the early years of all County Councils, the construction and maintenance of roads and bridges was important. Other functions of the County Council related to financing

Lee Fields flooded in November 2005 (picture: K. McCarthy).

Former Cork City Waterworks, now the Lifetime Lab, taken from the top of County Hall, June 2006 (picture: K. McCarthy).

county infirmaries, reformatory and industrial schools, coroners, courthouses, marine works, management of lunatic asylums, the eradication of diseases in animals, and contributing to agriculture and technical instruction. The first election for the Cork County Council took place on 6 April 1899. The term of office was three years.

From 1899 the council met at Cork City Courthouse and various departments of the council were scattered throughout the county. A site was purchased prior to the Second World War but with the rapid post war expansion of the local government services it was decided that the site, located in the city centre, was entirely inadequate. In 1953 the idea of central headquarters for the council's officers was mooted by Mr Joseph F. Wrenne, first County Manager. At the time, the times and costs were not considered. Mr Owen Callanan succeeded Mr Wrenne and he attained the council's approval, in principle, for one big roof for all of the council in 1954.

The original proposed building was to be 10 storeys high, 116 feet tall, 187 feet long and 42 feet high. Its long frontage was to face the Carrigrohane Road and it was to cost £137,000. The final plans differed from what was originally proposed. In the end the County Hall cost half a million pounds, was seventeen storeys high, 211 feet tall, 131 feet long and 46 feet wide, and its main entrance faced the city. Cork County Council acquired the site from John A. Wood. Previously, the greater part of the land was the headquarter grounds of the Munster Football Association. In 1964 the tender for the sum of £479,508 from Cork's largest firm of building contractors, Messrs P.J. Hegarty and Sons, Leitrim Street, was accepted for the construction of the seventeen-storey skyscraper, which was designed by Cork County Council Architect Patrick McSweeney.

Piling began on the bedrock about fifty feet below the surface in March 1965, and peak employment on the project was 120. All floors, with the exception of the uppermost, were

Left: Revamped Cork County Hall, June 2006 (picture: K. McCarthy).

Below: Former Our Lady's Hospital, now a major apartment complex in 2006, taken from the top of Cork County Hall (picture: K. McCarthy).

the same in section. This solved problems and minimised the costs of shuttering. Work commenced on the present site in 1965 and the hall was officially opened by Mr Martin Corry, TD, Chairman of Cork County Council, on 16 April 1968. The new Council Chamber was located on the sixteenth floor.

In recent times, County Hall has undergone an extension and redevelopment. An invited competition was organised by the Royal Institute of Architects of Ireland and the management team at Cork County Council for the general refurbishment of County Hall. Designed by Shay Cleary Architects, Dublin, the winning scheme provides an innovative solution to the façade of the tower by introducing a skin of glass louvres that respond to differing climatic conditions and allow the tower to provide a high-quality, naturally ventilated working environment.

(III) OUR LADY'S HOSPITAL — A CITY WITHIN A CITY:

While County Hall tower is the tallest building in Ireland, across the river is Ireland's longest building, the Mental Hospital. Built in Victorian times, it has now been renovated and converted into a residential housing complex. The first asylum for what contemporary Cork society deemed 'insane' people in Cork was founded under the Irish Gaol Act of 1787-1888. The Cork Asylum was the second of its kind to be established in Ireland and was to be part of the South Infirmary on Blackrock Road. The Cork Asylum in the late 1840s lacked finance and space to develop a proper institution. A Committee of the Grand Jury of Cork County (leading landlords and magistrates) examined the existing asylum and began a verbal campaign for its replacement. In 1845 a Westminster Act was enacted to create a District Asylum in Cork for the city and county of Cork.

In April 1846 the Board of Governors of the Asylum at the South Infirmary purchased and commenced work at a new site in Shanakiel. The board set up a competition of tender for an architectural design. Mr William Atkins was appointed, with Mr Alex Deane as builder. Work commenced in mid-1848. The new building was located on a commanding location on a steep hill, overlooking the Lee. The building was three floors high and was divided into four distinct blocks.

Three blocks were located at the front and were designed to contain the apartments for patients, along with the residences for the physicians, matron and other officials of the asylum. The building materials were reddish sandstone rubble, obtained near the site, and grey limestone quarried from sites from the opposite site of the Lee. Internal fittings such as fireplaces were said to be of marble supplied also from the south side of the city. The fourth building block was located at the rear of the central block, and comprised the kitchen, laundry, workshops, bakehouse, boiler house and other office rooms. Heating was steam-generated and came from a furnace house.

The new asylum was named Eglinton Lunatic Asylum after the Earl of Eglington, and was opened in 1852. Most people admitted were housewives, people from the labouring classes, servants, and the unemployed. Forty-two forms of lunacy were identified, produced by mental anxiety, grief, epilepsy, the death of a loved one, emigration, 'religious insanity', nervous depression, want of employment and desertion of husband or wife.

Plans for an extension to Eglington Asylum were put together in the 1870s. The aim was to accommodate over 1,300 patients. The three blocks were connected into a single building. In 1895, the Cork Asylum was described as one of the most modern asylums in Western Europe. Conditions in the institution were quite good. The staff included seventy-two men and fifty-six women. Lectures were given to staff by lecturers of mental illness at Queen's University College Cork, now University College Cork. A Church of Ireland chapel was completed in November 1885, with William Hill as the architect. In 1898 a Roman Catholic church was designed by Hill. In 1899, a new management committee for the asylum was established under the newly formed Cork

County Council. In 1926 the asylum became known as Cork District Mental Hospital. In 1952 the hospital's name was changed to Our Lady's Psychiatric Hospital. The complex closed in the late 1980s. In recent years, parts of the main grey building have been redeveloped into apartments.

The Lee Fields are an important crossroads, where the Lee's natural wildness and the urban wilderness of the city collide. There are many contrasts. On the one hand there is the Lee and its large flood plain, which can be seen regularly when the fields are waterlogged during Ireland's rainy conditions, or when the dam at Inniscarra is forced to release reservoir water. Different species of flora overhang the river and playful birds dive for fish. The slow current but heavy volume of water spills over the weir to meet the tidal water. On the other hand there are Cork's (Ireland's) most impressive buildings, such as the waterworks, Our Lady's Hospital, and the County Hall. Sites such as the Kingsley Hotel (formerly the site of the Lee Baths) and the new student accommodation are all located within view of the Lee fields and these reveal further insights into the past, present and future pulses of the city.

To be continued...

Divide at the river at the Lee fields into the South Channel and the North Channel, both of which extend through Cork City (picture: K. McCarthy).

BIBLIOGRAPHY

Aalen, F.H.A., Whelan, K. & Stout, M., 1997, *Atlas of the Irish Rural Landscape* (Cork University Press, Cork).

Ahern, M., *c.*2000, *Inniscarra Looks Back, Through the Avenues of Time* (St Colman's Press, Cork).

Ballincollig Community School, 1988, 'A Computerised Record of the History and Gravestones Inscriptions of St Peter's Church, Carrigrohane, Co. Cork', *Journal of the Ballincollig Community School*, Local History Society, Vol. 5.

Barry, T., 1949, *Guerrilla Days in Ireland* (Irish Press, Dublin).

Bartlett, W.H., *c.*1840, *The Scenery and Antiquities of Ireland* (George Virtue Publishing, London).

Brenneman, W.L. & Brenneman, M.G, 1995, *Crossing the Circle at the Holy Wells of Ireland*, Virgin Press, London.

Cody, B.A, 1859, *The River Lee, Cork and The Corkonians* (J. Barter & Sons, Cork).

Coleman, J.C., 1950, *Journeys into Muskerry* (Dundalgan Press, Dundalk).

Corkery, D., 1941, *The Hidden Ireland, A Study of Gaelic Munster in the Eighteenth Century* (M.H.Gill & Son, Dublin).

Cork City Library Files on Ballincollig, Co. Cork.

County Library Files on Ballincollig.

Creedon, C., 1985, *Cork City Railway Stations, 1849-1985: An Illustrated History* (Quality Print, Cork).

Croker, T.C., 1824, *Researches in the South of Ireland* (Cork).

Crookshank, A., 1978, 'A Sketch of Irish Landscape Painting', Eire.

Cross, E., 1941, *The Tailor and Ansty*, (Mercier Press Reprint, Cork).

Cusack, M., 1875, *A History of the City and County of Cork* (Messrs Bolster, Cork).

Donnelly, J., 1975, *The Land and the People of Nineteenth Century Cork* (Routledge & Kegan Paul, London).

Devoy, R., 2005, 'Cork City and The Evolution of the River Lee Valley' in Crowley, J.S., Devoy, R., Linehan, D. and O'Flangan, P. (Eds.), *Atlas of Cork City* (pages 7-16) (Cork University Press, Cork).

Dickson, D., 2005, *Old World Colony, Cork and South Munster, 1830-1830* (Cork University Press, Cork).

Donovan, D., 2005, *Ballincollig: A Local History* (Self published, Ballincollig).

Dwyer, F., 1997, *The Architecture of Deane and Woodward*, Cork University press, Cork.

E.S.B, 2006, *The River Lee Hydro Electric Scheme*, E.S.B. Educational Pack.

Farmer, D.H., 1975, *The Oxford Dictionary of Saints* (Oxford University Press, Oxford).

Fehily, P.C., 1980, *Cork Harbour and City Water Supply Scheme, Inniscarra Waterworks* (Cork County Council, Cork).

Foster, F., 1989, *The Oxford Illustrated History of Ireland* (Oxford University Press, Oxford).

Fitzgerald, J., c.1899, *Legends, Ballads and Songs of the Lee* (Hand-written, City Library).

Gibbings, R., 1945, *Lovely is the Lee* (J.M. Dent & Sons Ltd., London).

Gibson, C.B., 1861, (Reprint 1974), History of the County and City of Cork, (The Fercor Press, Cork).

Gordon, Col. 1811, Grand Jury Maps of Cork County.

Guy, 1891, *Cork City and County Directory*, (Guy & Co. Cork).

Griffith, R., 1853, *Primary Valuation of Tenements in the County of County Cork* (House of Commons, England)

Hart, P., 1998, *The I.R.A. and its Enemies, Violence and Community in Cork, 1916-1923* (Oxford Press, Oxford).

Healy, E. & Moriarty, C. & O'Flaherty, G, (Eds.), 1988, *The Book of the Liffey: From the Source to the Sea* (Wolfhound Press, Dublin).

Healy, E., 2001, *In Search of Ireland's Holy Wells* (Wolfhound Press, Dublin).

Healy, J.N., 1981, *Castles of County Cork* (Mercier Press, Cork).

Henry, H.M., 1989, *Our Lady's Hospital Cork, History of the Mental Hospital in Cork, Spanning 200 Years* (Haven Books, Cork).

Holland, M., 2 August 1930, 'Currykippane and J.J. Collins', *Cork Examiner*, p.13.

Interpretative Panels, Gearagh National Heritage Site.

Interpretative Panels, Kilmichael Ambush Site.

Interpretative Panels, The Aghinagh Way, Carrigadrohid.

Irwin, L., 1980, ' Politics, Religion and Economy: Cork in the 17th Century', *Journal of the Cork Historical and Archaeological Society*, vol. 85, page 6-25.

Irvine, J., 1964, *A Treasury of Irish Saints* (Dolmen Press, Oxford).

Jenkins, S.C., 1992, The Cork & Muskerry Light Railway (The Oakwood Press, Oxford).

Journals of the Ballingeary Historical Society, 1994-1996.

Kelleher, G.D, 1992, *The Gunpowder Mill at Ballincollig*, (John F. Kelleher, Inniscarra, Co. Cork).

Kerrigan, P., 1995, *Castles and Fortifications in Ireland, 1485-1945* (Collins Press, Cork).

Lewis, S., 1837, *Topographical Dictionary of Ireland* (Dublin).

Logan, P. 1980, *Holy Wells of Ireland* (Smythe Press, Dublin).

McCarthy, K., 2003, *Discover Cork*, (O'Brien Press, Dublin).

McGrath, W., 1981, *Tram Tracks of Cork* (Tower Books, Cork).

Meinig, D.W. (Ed.), 1979, *The Interpretation of Ordinary Landscapes, Geographical Landscapes* (Oxford University Press, Oxford).

Mitchell, F. & Ryan, D, 1986, *Reading the Irish Landscape* (Tower House and Country House Publishing, Dublin).

Murnane, E., *The First Hundred Years, 1899-1999*, Cork County Council (C.C.C. Publication, Cork).

Murray, P, 2004, *George Petrie (1790-1866), The Rediscovery of Ireland's Past* (Crawford Art Gallery with Gandon Editions, Kinsale, Co. Cork).

Ó Coindealbhain, S, c.1925, *The Story of Iveleary* (Dundalgan Press, Dundalk).

O'Donoghue, B., c.1990, *Parish Histories and Place Names of West Cork* (Kerryman Ltd., Co. Kerry).

O'Donoghue, S., 1996, *The Flooding of the Lee Valley* (Tower Books, Cork).

O'Faoláin, S., 1963, *Vive Moi !* (Sinclair-Stevenson Press, London).

O'Flanagan, J.R., 1944, *The Blackwater in Munster* (Tower Books reprint, Cork).
O'Keeffe, T., 1997, *Barryscourt Castle and the Irish Tower House*, (Gandon Editions / Barryscourt Trust, Cork).

O'Sullivan, A, 2000, *Crannógs, Lake-Dwellings of Early Ireland* (Town and Country House Ltd., Dublin).

Power, D. (Ed), 1995, *Archaeological Inventory of County Cork*, Mid Cork Volume (Government of Ireland Publications, Dublin).

Ring, D.P., 1995, *Macroom, Through the Mists of Time* (Castle House Publications, Macroom, Co. Cork).

Rynne, C., 1999, *The Industrial Archaeology of Cork City and its Environs* (Government of Ireland, Dublin).

Scott, Y., 2003, ' Refreshing the Landscape', *Irish Arts Review*, pages 60-61.

Snoddy, T, 2002, *Dictionary of Irish Artists* (Merlin Press, Dublin).

Smith, C., 1750, *A History of Cork* (Cork).

Strickland, W.G., 1969, *Dictionary of Irish Artists* (Irish University Press, Shannon).

Sweetnam, D., 1995, *Irish Castles and Fortified Houses* (Country House Press, Dublin).

The Kerryman Ltd. (Ed), 1947, *Rebel Cork's Fighting Story* (Kerryman Ltd, Co. Cork).

Townsend, H., 1815, *General and Statistical Survey of the County of Cork* (Edwards and Savage, Cork).

Windele, J., 1846, *Guide to the South of Ireland* (Messrs. Bolster, Cork).

Webb, J. & Donaldson, A, 2006, *Ballincollig Gunpowder Mills and Regional Park: A Hidden History,* (Nonsuch Ireland Ltd., Dublin).

Work of Dermot Lucey, History teacher, Ballincollig.